Greek and Roman Civilizations

Author: Heidi M. C. Dierckx, Ph.D.
Editors: Mary Dieterich and Sarah M. Anderson
Proofreader: Margaret Brown

COPYRIGHT © 2012 Mark Twain Media, Inc.

ISBN 978-1-58037-627-3

Printing No. CD-404161

Mark Twain Media, Inc., Publishers
Distributed by Carson-Dellosa Publishing LLC

Visit us at www.carsondellosa.com

Table of Contents

Introduction to the Teacher

The Western world owes much to the Greek and Roman civilizations, which laid the foundation for civilization in the West. Greek and Roman influence can be seen today in the areas of science, philosophy, government, literature, theater, art, and architecture. In order to understand our world today, it is necessary to study the impact of the Greek and Roman civilizations of the past.

Greek and Roman Civilizations is specifically designed to facilitate planning for the diverse learning styles and skills levels of middle-school students. The special features of the book provide the teacher with alternative methods of instruction. A modified version of the text is available for download for struggling readers.

Book Features:

- **Reading Selection** introduces facts and information as a reading exercise.

- **Knowledge Check** assesses student understanding of the reading exercise using selected response and constructed response questioning strategies.

- **Map Follow-Up** provides opportunities for students to report information from a spatial perspective.

- **Explore** allows students to expand learning by participating in high-interest, hands-on and research activities.

Online Resources:

Reluctant Reader Text: A modified version of the reading exercise pages can be downloaded from the website at www.carsondellosa.com. In the Search box, enter the product code CD-404161. When you reach the *Greek and Roman Civilizations* product page, click the icon for the Reluctant Reader Text download.

The readability level of the text has been modified to facilitate struggling readers. The Flesch-Kincaid Readability formula, which is built into Microsoft Word™, was used to determine the readability level. The formula calculates the number of words, syllables, and sentences in each paragraph, producing a reading level.

Additional Resources:

Classroom decoratives appeal to visual learners. The *Greek and Roman Civilizations* Bulletin Board Set, available from Mark Twain Media, Inc., can be used to visually reinforce lessons found in this book in an interesting and attention-grabbing way. The *Eastern Hemisphere Maps* or *World Geography: Middle-East Maps* Bulletin Board Sets are also helpful when studying the geography of the Greek and Roman civilizations.

Greek and Roman Time Lines

DATES IN GREEK HISTORY
ALL DATES B.C.

c. 3000	Beginning of Minoan civilization on Crete
c. 2000–1450	Palace period: building of palaces at Knossos and other places
c. 1450	Destruction of palaces: end of Minoan power
	Volcanic eruption of Thera
c. 1400–1200	Height of Mycenaean civilization: building of palaces at Mycenae and other places
c. 1220 (?)	Trojan War (?)
c. 1200–1150	Destruction of Mycenaean palaces
	Dorian Invasion (?)
c. 1200–750	Dark Age
	Introduction of iron
c. 1050–950	Ionian Migrations
c. 750	Start of Hellenic civilization: rise of city-states, introduction of alphabet, trade increases
776	Traditional date for the first Olympic Games
750–600	Greek colonization
650–500	Rise of tyrannies
594	Solon starts the process of democracy in Athens
560–527	Reign of Peisistratus of Athens
546	Cyrus, king of Persia, conquers Asia Minor, including the Asiatic Greeks
508–507	Cleisthenes' reforms in Athens
by 500	Foundation of Peloponnesian League
499–494	Ionian Revolt
490–479	Persian Wars
490	Persian invasion of Greece under King Darius
	Battle of Marathon
483	Themistocles builds new Athenian fleet
480	King Xerxes invades Greece
	Battle of Thermopylae
	Battle of Salamis
479	Battle of Plataea
	Battle of Mycale
478	Foundation of Delian League
468	Final defeat of Persians at Battle of Euremedon (Asia Minor)
461–429	Rule of Pericles in Athens
431–421	Peloponnesian War I
415–404	Peloponnesian War II
411	Oligarchic Revolution in Athens
405	Battle of Aegospotami: defeat of Athens
404–403	Rule of the Thirty Tyrants in Athens

404–371	Supremacy of Sparta
386	King's Peace
371	Battle of Leuctra: Theban victory
371–362	Supremacy of Thebes; rule of Epaminondas at Thebes
362	Battle of Mantinea: Spartan and Athenian victory
359–336	Rule of Philip II of Macedonia
338	Battle of Chaeronea: Philip II conquers the Greeks
336–323	Rule of Alexander the Great
336–30	Hellenistic civilization
334	Battle at Granikos River
333	Battle at Issos River
331	Battle of Gaugamela: end of Persian power
	Alexander the Great becomes King of the Greeks and the Persians
323	Alexander the Great dies in Babylon

> **"Fair Greece! sad relic of departed worth!**
> **Immortal, though no more! though fallen, great!"**
>
> **[Lord Byron, "Childe Harold's Pilgrimage" (1812–1818), canto 2, stanza 73]**

DATES IN ROMAN HISTORY
The Monarchy and Republic Period
ALL DATES B.C.

753	Foundation of Rome
	Kings: Romulus
	Numa Pompilius
	Tullus Hostilius
	Ancus Martius
	Tarquinius Priscus
	Servius Tullius
	Tarquinius Superbus
509	Start of the Roman Republic
494–287	Patrician-Plebeian social struggle
390	Gauls sack Rome
390–338	War with the Latins (Latium)
4th century	War with the Etruscans and other Italic tribes
343–290	Samnite Wars
287	Lex Hortensia
280–275	War with Pyrrhus
264–241	First Punic War; Sicily and Sardinia become the first Roman province
218–201	Second Punic War
216	Battle of Cannae
202	Battle of Zama; Spain becomes two Roman provinces

200–196	War in Greece
171–168	War in Greece
149–146	Third Punic War
146	Destruction of Corinth and Carthage
133	Pergamon becomes a province of Asia
	Reforms and death of Tiberius Gracchus
123	Reforms of Gaius Gracchus (killed 121 B.C.)
88	Sulla marches on Rome
87	Marius retakes Rome (dies 86 B.C.)
82	First civil war; Sulla becomes dictator (dies 78 B.C.)
73–71	Spartacus' slave revolt
70	Crassus and Pompey are consuls
63	Annexation of Syria and other areas as Roman provinces
60	First Triumvirate: alliance of Caesar, Pompey, and Crassus
58–51	Caesar in Gaul; Gallic Wars
53	Death of Crassus
49–46	Second civil war; Caesar becomes dictator
44	Death of Caesar
43	Second Triumvirate: Octavian, Mark Antony, and Lepidus
42	Death of Brutus and Cassius at Philippi
31	Battle of Actium: Octavian defeats forces of Antony and Cleopatra and becomes sole ruler of the Republic

THE ROMAN EMPIRE
Emperors
Julio-Claudian Dynasty

27 B.C.–A.D. 14	*Augustus* (new name of Octavian)

ALL DATES THAT FOLLOW ARE A.D.

14–37	*Tiberius*
37–41	*Caligula*
41–54	*Claudius*
43	Invasion of Britain
54–68	*Nero*
64	Great fire of Rome
69	Civil war

Flavian Dynasty

69–79	*Vespasian*
79–81	*Titus*
79	Eruption of Vesuvius: Pompeii and Herculaneum destroyed
81–96	*Domitian*

The "Five Good Emperors"

96–98	*Nerva*
98–117	*Trajan*
117–138	*Hadrian*

138–161	*Antoninus Pius*
161–180	*Marcus Aurelius*
	End of the Pax Romana
180–192	*Commodus*
193	Civil war

Severan Dynasty

193–211	*Septimius Severus*
211–217	*Caracalla* and *Geta*
217–218	*Macrinus*
218–222	*Elagabalus*
222–235	*Severus Alexander*
235–284	Civil war; many emperors ruled at the same time
284–305	*Diocletian* and *Maximian*
	Empire split into East and West
	Formation of the tetrarchy
301	Edict of prices
303–311	Great Persecution of Christians
306–337	*Constantine the Great:* first Christian emperor
311	Edict of Sophia: tolerance of all religions
312	Battle at the Milvian Bridge
313	Edict of Milan: in favor of Christianity
325	Council of Nicaea
330	Foundation of Constantinople
337	Constantine the Great baptized a Christian
360–363	*Julian the Apostate;* restoration of paganism
364–375	*Valentinian I* rules the West
364–378	*Valens* rules the East
378	Battle of Adrianople; Valens killed by Visigoths
379–395	*Theodosius I;* last emperor of a united empire
395	Christianity becomes the official state religion
	Permanent split of the empire into East and West
452	Attila the Hun invades Italy and is halted by Pope Leo I
475–476	*Romulus Augustulus:* last Roman emperor in the West
476	End of the Western Roman Empire
	Odovacer deposes Romulus Augustulus and is proclaimed King of Italy

> **"NESCIRE AUTEM, QUID ANTEA, QUAM NATUS SIS,**
> **ACCIDERIT, ID EST SEMPER ESSE PUERUM"**
> **CICERO (ORATIONS, 34)**
>
> **"NOT TO KNOW WHAT HAPPENED BEFORE**
> **ONE WAS BORN, IS ALWAYS TO BE A CHILD."**

The Greek Alphabet

Greek is one of the languages that belongs to the Indo-European language family that includes German, English, and Italian. The alphabet, from which our own alphabet is derived through Greek and Latin, was first developed by the Phoenicians, a seafaring people who lived on the coast of present-day Lebanon between 1200 and 800 B.C. The Phoenician alphabet consisted of 22 consonants. About 750 B.C. the Greeks took over the Phoenician alphabet and modified it to suit their language. Because the Phoenician alphabet did not have separate characters for the vowels, the Greeks adapted and systematized vowels signs. The Greek alphabet has 24 letters. While many of them look familiar, the letters are written in a different way than our own letters, which were derived from the Latin alphabet.

Letter		Name	Latin equivalent
lower case	upper case		
α	A	alpha	a (as in father)
β	B	beta	b
γ	Γ	gamma	g
δ	Δ	delta	d
ε	E	epsilon	e
ζ	Z	zeta	z
η	H	eta	e (as in send)
θ	Θ	theta	th
ι	I	iota	i (as in mint)
κ	K	kappa	k
λ	Λ	lambda	l
μ	M	mu	m
ν	N	nu	n
ξ	Ξ	xi	x (as in example)
o	O	omicron	o (as in lot)
π	Π	pi	p
ρ	P	rho	r
σ, ς	Σ	sigma	s
τ	T	tau	t
υ	Y	upsilon	u
φ	Φ	phi	ph
χ	X	chi	ch
ψ	Ψ	psi	ps
ω	Ω	omega	o (as in photo)

Name: _____   Date: _____

The Latin Alphabet and Numerals

Like Greek, Latin belongs to the Indo-European language family. The Latin alphabet was adopted from the Greek alphabet by way of the Etruscans. Our own alphabet is directly derived from the Latin alphabet. The Latin alphabet consisted of 23 letters. The letters J, U, and W were added later to our alphabet. In Latin, the letters I and V were used both as vowels and consonants and were used to write and pronounce the letters J, U, and W. The Romans used only capital letters to write their language. Lower-case letters did not appear until the Middle Ages. The Latin alphabet is:

A B C D E F G H I K L M N O P Q R S T V X Y Z

The Romans wrote numbers by using seven signs of the alphabet:

$$
\begin{aligned}
\text{I} &= 1 \\
\text{V} &= 5 \\
\text{X} &= 10 \\
\text{L} &= 50 \\
\text{C} &= 100 \\
\text{D} &= 500 \\
\text{M} &= 1000
\end{aligned}
$$

The numbers are written next to each other in descending order and are added up.

For example: II = 2; VI = 6; LXVIII = 68.

However, if a smaller number is written in front of a larger number, the smaller number is subtracted from the larger number.

For example: IX = 9; IV = 4; XC = 90.

The year 1995 is written MCMXCV.

Translate the following Roman numerals into Arabic numerals (the numerals we use today).

1. LXXXVIII   _____
2. MMIX   _____
3. DCCII   _____
4. DCLXI   _____
5. CMXXX   _____

6. XVIII   _____
7. XLIV   _____
8. CCCLXXIII   _____
9. CDLVI   _____
10. LXXXIX   _____

Latin Phrases and Quotations
Used in the English Language

Phrases	Translation
alter ego	one's second self
a posteriori	inductive reasoning; from effect to cause
a priori	deductive reasoning; from cause to effect
bona fide	good faith
carpe diem	seize the day; enjoy the moment
cogito, ergo sum	I think, therefore I am
de facto	existing by fact, not by right
et alia (et al.)	and other things
et cetera (etc.)	and the rest
exampli gratia (e.g.)	for example
ex gratia	performed as an act of grace
ibidem (ibid.)	the same text
idem	the same
id est (i.e.)	that is
in excelsis	in the highest
in principio	in the beginning
in situ	in the original place
inter alia	among other things
ipso facto	by the fact itself
nota bene	note well
persona (non)grata	an (un)acceptable person
quid pro quo	this for that
sine qua non	fundamental cause; necessary precondition
verbatim	word for word; exactly as quoted

Quotations	Translation
ad praesens ova cras pullis sunt meliora	eggs today are better than chickens tomorrow
ave, Caesar, morituri te salutant	Hail Caesar, those of us who are about to die salute you
veni, vidi, vici (Julius Caesar)	I came, I saw, I conquered
aut disce aut discede (Oxford)	either learn or leave
dum vivimus, viviamus	while we live, let us live
felix qui nihil debet	happy is he who owes nothing
nam et ipsa scientia potestas est (Bacon)	for knowledge is itself power
non semper ea sunt quae videntur (Phaedrus)	things are never what they seem
nosce te ipsum	know thyself
respice, adspice, prospice	look to the past, look to the present, look to the future
temporis ars medicina fere est (Ovid)	time is the best means of healing

Knossos

Legend of King Minos

Legend tells of a **King Minos** who lived on the island of Crete in the Aegean Sea. In his palace at Knossos he had a **labyrinth** (maze) where a mythical beast, called the **Minotaur**, lived. This beast had the head of a bull and the body of a human. Annually, the king of Athens had to send seven young men and seven young maidens to King Minos as food for the Minotaur. One year, Theseus, son of the

This fresco depicts the sport of bull-leaping, which was popular with the people of Crete.

king of Athens, accompanied the young victims to Crete. After arriving at Knossos, Theseus and his companions were helped by Ariadne, King Minos' daughter, who gave him a dagger to kill the Minotaur and some thread to find his way out of the labyrinth. And so Theseus killed the beast, found his way safely out of the labyrinth, and freed Athens from the annual obligation of sending fourteen youths to Crete.

Discovering the Minoan Civilization

In A.D. 1900 a famous British archaeologist named Arthur Evans discovered a large palace at **Knossos** in north-central Crete. This palace belonged to a civilization that Evans called the **Minoan civilization**, named after the legendary King Minos of the labyrinth. This civilization flourished on Crete between 2000 and 1450 B.C. (See map on page 18.)

The Minoan civilization consisted of a number of palaces, the largest of which is located at Knossos. The palace had several purposes. It served as the residence of the king, who was the supreme ruler, along with his family and attendants. It was also a place where attendants and higher officials carried out the daily business of the palace and the area it controlled. Finally, food and trade items were stored there and redistributed to the common people of the countryside.

The Minoan people lived in towns and villages. Some cultivated primarily olives and grapes. Others were craftsmen and artisans. They manufactured luxury items, such as finely painted pottery, elaborately carved stone vessels, and jewelry. These items were traded as far away as Egypt and the Near East. Trade was an important part of Minoan life. This civilization was prosperous and technologically advanced. The palaces had an advanced drainage system complete with baths. **Frescoes**, or wall paintings, decorated the walls of the palaces with scenes of animals, games, and religious festivals. This indicates that the Minoans were a peaceful and fun-loving people. The Minoans loved games, such as boxing and bull-leaping. **Bull-leaping** involved jumping onto a bull by grabbing its horns, doing a somersault, and landing back on the ground.

The End of the Minoan Civilization

About 1450 B.C. the Minoan civilization came to an end. The palaces and towns were destroyed. Archaeologists can only guess as to the cause of this destruction. About fifty years before, a volcano on the nearby island of Thera had erupted violently. It brought large amounts of ash and tidal waves to Crete. As a result, it is believed that the Aegean trading system, as well as Minoan food production, was disrupted. Today, only the ancient ruins of this once wealthy and advanced civilization remain.

Name: _____ Date: _____

Knowledge Check

Matching

_____ 1. labyrinth

_____ 2. frescoes

_____ 3. Minoan civilization

_____ 4. King Minos

_____ 5. Knossos

_____ 6. Minotaur

_____ 7. bull-leaping

a. legendary ruler of the island of Crete

b. location of a large palace on Crete

c. a maze

d. culture living on Crete named after King Minos

e. beast with the head of a bull and the body of a human

f. game where a person jumped over a bull, did a somersault, and landed on the ground

g. wall paintings

Multiple Choice

8. Who discovered the Minoan civilization in 1900?

    a. Theseus

    c. Heinrich Schleimann

    b. Arthur Evans

    d. Julius Caesar

9. What items were NOT grown or made by the Minoans as far as we know?

    a. pottery

    c. olives

    b. jewelry

    d. weapons

Constructed Response

10. What kind of evidence, or lack of evidence, found on Crete tells us that the Minoans can be considered a peaceful and fun-loving people? Use details from the reading selection to support your answer.

_____

_____

_____

_____

_____

_____

Mycenae

The Lion Gate at Mycenae

The Mycenaean Civilization

Homer, the first known Greek poet, who lived about 700 B.C., wrote of another civilization that arose after the fall of the Minoan civilization. It was called the **Mycenaean civilization**. In his epic, the *Iliad,* Homer described the wealthy palaces where heroic kings, such as Agamemnon of Mycenae, lived. These kings waged war against the people of Troy, a walled city located on the coast of northern Turkey, on the east side of the Aegean. According to the story, the Mycenaeans defeated the Trojans in a battle inside the city walls after hiding inside a large wooden horse (the **Trojan Horse**), which the Trojans were tricked into bringing inside the city gates.

This civilization was named after an important palace, Mycenae, located in the **Peloponnese** on mainland Greece (the southern region of Greece connected to the rest of the country by the Isthmus of Corinth). (See map on page 18.) It was discovered by a famous German archaeologist Heinrich Schliemann in A.D. 1876. The Mycenaeans were Greeks who came to the Greek mainland about 2000 B.C. By about 1500 B.C., there emerged a civilization as prosperous and wealthy as that of Minoan Crete.

Archaeological Evidence of Mycenae

The archaeological remains in the Peloponnese consist of large palaces that served the same purposes as those found on Crete. Unlike the Minoans, however, the Mycenaeans were a warlike people. The palaces were surrounded by well-built walls for defense. The frescoes on the walls show many scenes of hunting and warfare. **Bronze** weapons and body armor and helmets made of ivory tusks were also found among the artifacts. For survival in case of siege, the Mycenaeans built underground tunnels leading to a water well outside the palace gates. Like the Minoans, the Mycenaeans cultivated olives and grapes and traded jars of oil and wine, as well as painted pottery, throughout the Mediterranean region.

Mycenaeans buried their dead in monumental family tombs. The burial chamber of the tomb was dug into a hillside and was approached by a long tunnel-like entrance (called a *dromos*). The dead were buried with their belongings (painted pottery, gold jewelry and cups, and weapons) on the floor or in a pit of the chamber.

The End of the Mycenaean Civilization

The Mycenaeans had a written language, which was written on rectangular clay tablets. The script is called **"Linear B"** because its characters consisted of lines. The tablets contain lists of food and other products made, stored, and distributed by the palace officials. They contain no historical information that can tell us of any wars or the reason for the end of this civilization. Disaster struck the palaces between about 1200 and 1100 B.C. They were destroyed by fire, and the people abandoned their homes. Many causes could have contributed to the fall of this civilization: drought, civil war, or outside invaders from the north called the Dorians. There is no evidence, however, to tell us exactly what happened.

Name: _____ Date: _____

Knowledge Check

Matching

_____ 1. Peloponnese

_____ 2. Homer

_____ 3. Mycenaean civilization

_____ 4. bronze

_____ 5. dromos

_____ 6. Trojan Horse

_____ 7. Linear B

a. metal used to make weapons and body armor

b. language consisting of lines written on clay tablets

c. long tunnel-like entrance to a burial chamber

d. the first known Greek poet

e. wooden horse the Mycenaeans hid inside during the war with Troy

f. southern region of Greece connected to the rest of the country by the Isthmus of Corinth

g. civilization named after an important palace in the Peloponnese region of Greece

Multiple Choice

8. Which of the following is NOT a possible cause of the end of the Mycenaean civilization?

   a. ice-age climate change
   b. drought
   c. invaders called Dorians
   d. civil war

9. What did the Mycenaeans build to survive a siege in times of war?

   a. a large wooden horse
   b. a large palace
   c. tunnels leading to a water well
   d. tunnels leading to a burial chamber

Constructed Response

10. What evidence exists to tell us that the Mycenaeans were a warlike people? Use details from the reading selection to support your answer.

_____

_____

_____

_____

_____

_____

_____

The Rise of Hellenic Civilization

The Dark Ages

During the four centuries B.C. following the Mycenaean civilization, Greece fell into a period of decline. The prosperity and wealth of the Mycenaean period had gone. The flourishing arts, monumental architecture, and knowledge of writing disappeared. Trade declined, and the Mycenaean palaces were abandoned. The period is known as the "**Dark Ages**," and it lasted from about 1200 to 750 B.C.

Homer, who wrote about the heroic deeds of Mycenaean kings in the *Iliad,* also described the events within the social and political background of this dark period. Agriculture had returned to a simple level of **subsistence**. Every man owned and cultivated his own small plot of land for individual survival. The king was no longer the supreme and authoritative ruler, but was advised in regard to what action should be taken by a small group of nobles or aristocrats. The **monarchy** of the Mycenaean period, where

Homer wrote about the period in Greek history known as the Dark Ages.

the king was supreme, was replaced by a "rule of a few men," called an **oligarchy**. A small group of wealthy nobles had all the power.

Another significant change that occurred at the beginning of this period was the introduction of iron for making tools and weapons. Accordingly, this period is also known as the "**Iron Age**."

The Ionian Migrations

One major event that characterizes the "Dark Ages" was a migration of Greeks across the Aegean Sea. Thucydides, a fifth century B.C. Greek historian, called this the **Ionian Migrations**. (See map on page 18.) Three groups of Greeks, based on dialects they spoke, moved to and settled on the western coast of **Asia Minor** (modern-day Turkey). The Dorians, who spoke Doric, settled in the southern part; the Ionians, who spoke Ionic, inhabited the middle part; and the Aeolians, who spoke Aeolic, went to the northern part of the area. The Greeks living in this coastal area were later to be the cause of conflict between the Greeks and the Persians.

Hellenic Civilization

By the middle of the eighth century B.C., Greece had recovered from its darkest period in history, and a new civilization emerged. This was called the **Hellenic** (or Greek) civilization. Trade once again began to flourish. The alphabet was introduced into Greece from Phoenicia, a seafaring state located in today's Lebanon. Because the alphabet contained no vowels, vowels were added to adapt to the Greek language. Most importantly, a new political institution emerged, which typified the rest of Greek political history—the **city-state** or *polis*. Because Greece is a very mountainous region, small independent political units developed rather than a large political union. Another factor in the development of city-states was the Greeks' love for freedom and independence. Each city-state was autonomous with its own laws and constitution, leaders and army, system of taxation, and sometimes its own coinage system. The largest and most important of Greek city-states were Athens in Attica, Sparta in the Peloponnese, and Thebes in Boeotia.

Until about 650 B.C., most city-states were ruled by the aristocrats. They had an oligarchic form of government. The political power was in the hands of a few wealthy families who owned the best land and abused the majority of the city-state's citizens who were poor farmers. Sometimes these farmers got into debt and were forced to work for the aristocrats to pay off their debts. Some even became slaves.

Greek Colonization

Starting about 750 B.C., due to poverty and insufficient farming land, these poor farmers began to leave their homelands and seek new opportunities elsewhere. Other reasons for emigration, even though less important, were trade, personal adventure, and political refuge. A phase of **"Greek colonization"** was launched. (See inset map on page 18.) Colonies were set up along the coasts of southern Italy and Sicily (known as Magna Graecia or Greater Greece), France, Spain, and along the coast of the northern Aegean and Black Seas. Some important colonies include Syracuse (Sicily), Phaestum and Cumae (Italy), Massalia (modern Marseille, France), and Byzantium on the Black Sea (modern Istanbul). The Greek city-states that took part in this colonization process were mostly Athens, Corinth in the Peloponnese, Eretria and Chalkis on the island of Euboea, and the Greek-Asiatic cities of Miletus and Phocaea. The Greek colonies became city-states of their own and were politically and economically independent. The only ties that remained with their mother city-states were cultural and religious. By 600 B.C. the Greeks had spread their people and ideas throughout the regions of the Mediterranean and Black Seas. This Greek influence was later to have a profound effect on Roman culture.

Tyrannies

One of the results of Greek colonization was the emergence of a new social class of people, the middle class or merchants, who had become wealthy through industry and trade. This new middle class also wanted a share in the political power of the city-states. Consequently, at home in Greece, the discontent of the poor was solved in another way. Tyrants, men from the new middle class, came to power in many city-states between 650 and 500 B.C. with the support of the people. This type of government is called a **tyranny**. A Greek **tyrant**, however, unlike today's tyrant, was not a brutal ruler, but a ruler who had not taken power according to the constitution. In fact, most Greek tyrants were good rulers and brought many benefits, such as power and wealth, to the city-states. Coinage was introduced, trade and colonization were encouraged, and athletic, musical, and dramatic contests were established. One notable tyrant was Peisistratus of Athens (560–529 B.C.), who embellished the city with monuments, stimulated trade and industry, and helped the poor farmers. He increased the prestige of Athens.

A very important change that took place during this time, and one which may also have helped the rise in power of tyrants, was the development of an infantry army. A new type of heavily armed soldier called a *hoplite*, placed within a tight formation, called a *phalanx*, fought many successful battles for the next three centuries.

Democracy

The rule of tyrannies did not last very long, however, because some of the tyrants in power became too authoritarian. Instead, the governments of the city-states became once again oligarchies or changed to a new form of rule, **democracy**. Democracy, or "rule by the people," was first developed in Athens. Sparta, on the other hand, retained a form of oligarchic rule. The other Greek city-states followed the lead of either Athens or Sparta.

Hoplite

Name: _____ Date: _____

Knowledge Check

Matching

_____ 1. subsistence
_____ 2. monarchy
_____ 3. oligarchy
_____ 4. tyranny
_____ 5. democracy
_____ 6. city-state
_____ 7. hoplite
_____ 8. phalanx
_____ 9. Hellenic

a. rule by the people
b. rule by a man who had not taken power according to the constitution
c. rule by a few wealthy men
d. rule by a king
e. Greek
f. farming a small plot of land for individual survival
g. a tight formation of soldiers
h. a heavily armed Greek soldier
i. a small independent political unit based around a city; polis

Multiple Choice

10. During the Dark Ages, Greeks migrated across the Aegean Sea to _____.

     a. Italy   b. Asia Minor   c. Egypt   d. Massalia

11. During the Greek colonization period, what new social class of people emerged?

     a. slaves   b. aristocrats   c. upper class   d. middle class

Constructed Response

12. Why did the Hellenic civilization develop the political institution of the city-state or polis? Use details from the reading selection to support your answer.

     _____

     _____

     _____

     _____

     _____

     _____

     _____

     _____

Lycurgus and Sparta

Heavily armed hoplites became the backbone of Greek armies.

Lycurgus Establishes Spartan Institutions

According to the Spartans, about 700 B.C. a semi-legendary figure named **Lycurgus** established a number of social and political institutions that made Sparta a great power of Greece.

He started an educational system that produced men of military strength and loyal soldiers. It all began at birth. If a newly born baby was weak or sickly, it was abandoned and left to die on a mountain slope. At the age of seven, a boy came under the control of the city and remained so until his death. He was to live together with the other boys in a camp, and the training process started. The boys learned to read and write and were taught music and poetry. Most importantly, however, they were taught discipline, courage, and virtue. Each boy exercised a lot and competed in violent games and fights. They were forced to steal, but if caught, the boys were punished for being careless and unskillful. Their training continued into manhood. The girls were also brought up in a strict manner. They had to exercise their bodies to make them grow strong in order to be able to deal easily with childbirth.

The Spartan Economy

Sparta did not adopt a **coinage** system like other Greek cities because wealth was not desirable and was regarded without envy and prestige. Trade was forbidden both within and outside the city. Every citizen had an equal share of land to live on. They were also forbidden to travel, except on army expeditions during times of war, in order that they might not be exposed to foreign behaviors and ideas. The Spartans were very patriotic Greeks and fought for their state until their death. They had adopted a system of living where there was little individual freedom and where order and discipline ruled.

Government in Sparta

Lycurgus also set up a type of government at Sparta that was a form of oligarchy. A few wealthy aristocrats held the power, but the city's constitution retained its kings of the previous age. No individual was able to become too powerful. The government consisted of two *kings* who were the generals of the army. The executive power lay in the hands of five **magistrates**, called *ephors*. The ephors were the judges of the city and dealt with internal and foreign affairs. They obtained advice from the **council of elders**, which consisted of 28 ex-magistrates. A second council of the Spartan people (*Spartiates*), called the **assembly**, also existed. This council had the right to reject or approve any proposals put before them.

Social Groups in Sparta

Sparta controlled about two-fifths of the Peloponnese. During the eighth century B.C., Sparta conquered Laconia and Messenia and their inhabitants. (See map on page 18.) In the Spartan social structure, these inhabitants were divided into two groups: the *helots*, who were slaves who worked the land to supply food for the Spartiates, and the *perioiki*, who were freedmen but were socially inferior. Both groups would also have to join the Spartan army in times of war.

Name: _____ Date: _____

Knowledge Check

Matching

_____ 1. coinage

_____ 2. Spartiates

_____ 3. helots

_____ 4. perioiki

_____ 5. magistrates

_____ 6. ephors

_____ 7. assembly

a. freedmen who were socially inferior

b. a council of Spartan people who could reject or approve proposals put before them

c. judges

d. the Spartan people

e. slaves who worked the land to supply food for the Spartiates

f. a system of money

g. judges of the city who dealt with internal and foreign affairs

Multiple Choice

8. Which of the following was NOT something Spartan boys learned?

    a. reading and writing   b. stealing

    c. music and poetry   d. banking

9. Which group of people would have to join the Spartan army in times of war?

    a. ephors   b. helots

    c. Spartan women   d. elders

Constructed Response

10. Why were the Spartans not allowed to trade or travel? How do you think this may have affected Sparta culturally and economically? Use details from the reading selection to support your answer.

_____

_____

_____

_____

_____

_____

_____

Athens and Democracy

Government in Athens

The oligarchy of Sparta was radically different from the type of government practiced by the Athenians, who set up a **democracy**. The constitution was not in the hands of the few; rather, it was controlled by the many—the **demos** or people.

Solon

Four men were responsible for the development of democracy in Athens. Solon, in 594 B.C., was the first. He made social and political reforms to lessen the conflict

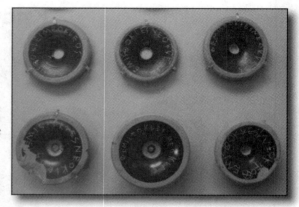

Examples of ostraka (potshards) cast against Themistocles

between the rich and poor in the city. In order to free all citizens from debt and enslavement, he cancelled all debts and abolished slavery. Politically, he reduced the power of the wealthy aristocrats by giving more power to the people.

The government already consisted of two leaders called **archons** who held the executive power. These men were advised by an aristocratic council of elders called the Council of the Areopagus (the **Areopagus** was a hill in Athens where its meetings were held). To these Solon now added three new political bodies that gave more power to the average citizen: a People's Court where all disputes, public or private, were settled by the people; the People's Assembly (to which all Athenian citizens belonged) that decided on the matters of the state; and a Council of 400 (which consisted of 100 citizens from each of the four tribes that made up the Athenian citizenry) that prepared business for the Assembly to consider. Solon's reforms, however, pleased neither the populace, because not enough power was given, nor the aristocrats, because their power was decreased. Unrest followed.

Peisistratus

Peisistratus then became tyrant in 560 B.C. Among his benefits to the city, he continued the process of democratization by **redistributing** the land (previously owned by the rich nobles) to farmers and making loans to poor farmers to start anew.

Cleisthenes

In 508 B.C. a third influential figure, Cleisthenes, came to power in Athens. He did much to develop Athenian democracy. Cleisthenes divided the citizens into ten new tribes (from the four old tribes) and mixed them up so that no one tribe was dominated by the rich as had been the case before. He increased the Council of 400 to the Council of 500, which now consisted of 50 citizens from each tribe. He also introduced the practice of **ostracism**. Every year the Athenians could banish from the city any man they deemed threatening. This was done by writing his name on a potshard or **ostraka**. The man with the most votes was then exiled for ten years.

Pericles

It was in the time of Pericles (461–429 B.C.), one of Athens' best statesmen, that democracy was completely attained. He made all offices in the government payable, and all officers were elected by lot rather than by vote, so that even the poorest citizens now could participate in the government.

Athenian democracy has influenced many democratic goverments in world history, including the American governmental system.

Name: _____ Date: _____

Knowledge Check

Matching

_____ 1. archons
_____ 2. Areopagus
_____ 3. democracy
_____ 4. demos
_____ 5. ostracism
_____ 6. ostraka
_____ 7. redistributing

a. potshards that people used to cast votes
b. rule by the people
c. taking land from rich nobles and dividing it up among farmers
d. the people
e. voting to banish any man deemed threatening
f. the hill in Athens where the council of elders met
g. two leaders who held executive power in Athens

Multiple Choice

8. Who was the first Athenian leader to start the process of democracy?

   a. Cleisthenes   b. Peisistratus
   c. Pericles   d. Solon

9. By mixing up the citizens in the tribes, Cleisthenes wanted to prevent the _____ from dominating any one tribe.

   a. soldiers   b. rich
   c. farmers   d. archons

Constructed Response

10. What differences and similarities do you see between the Spartan and Athenian governments? Use details from this reading selection and the one on Sparta to support your answer.

_____

_____

_____

_____

_____

_____

_____

The Wars With Persia

Greek trireme

The Persians

About 1000 B.C., an Indo-European people called the Persians occupied the area east of the Tigris River in western Asia. They became a powerful nation during the sixth century B.C. under King Cyrus the Great (559–529 B.C.). Cyrus not only made Persia a strong empire in western Asia, but also expanded Persian rule to include most of western Asia up to the Indus River. The Greek cities on the western coast of Asia Minor were also conquered by Cyrus and became subjects of the Persians. His sons, Cambyses (529–522 B.C.) and Darius (522–486 B.C.), who succeeded him on the throne of Persia, expanded the empire to include Egypt and northern Greece. By about 500 B.C., Persia extended from the Mediterranean Sea in the west to the edge of India in the east and from the Black Sea in the north to the Persian Gulf in the south. (See map on page 21.) It was organized into 20 provinces called **satrapies**, each ruled by a **satrap** or governor. Trade and communication were made efficient (and thus aided in the ruling of the empire) by the building of the **Royal Road**, which ran from the first capital city, Sousa, to Sardis. Not much later, the capital was moved to Persepolis under King Xerxes (486–465 B.C.), son of Darius.

The Ionian Revolt

The Greeks in Asia Minor were not very happy under Persian rule and wanted freedom. Therefore, they decided to revolt against their foreign rulers in 499 B.C. Thus began the **Ionian Revolt**, which was the beginning of the fighting between the Greeks and Persians, known as the Persian Wars. The Persian Wars were described in detail by the first known Greek historian, Herodotus, in the fifth century B.C. The Ionian Revolt was started by Aristagoras, tyrant of the Greek city of Miletus, who spurred on the other Ionian cities to rise up against the Persians. (See map on page 18.) The Ionian Greeks, realizing they needed help from the mainland Greeks to accomplish their goal, asked both Sparta and Athens for ships and men. Only Athens and its ally Eretria in Euboea were willing to help, and they sent out 25 manned ships. The aid, however, was too little, and after a major defeat, the Greek allies were forced to withdraw. The uprising ended when Miletus was sacked by the Persians in 494 B.C. The revolt had failed, and the Ionian Greeks were back under Persian control. However, as Herodotus said, this incident was the beginning of trouble for both the Greeks and the Persians.

Persian Wars, Battle of Marathon

Darius, King of the Persians at this time, partially intending to punish the Athenians for their aid to the Asiatic Greeks and partially to expand Persian rule into Europe, decided to invade mainland Greece. This first expedition occurred in 492 B.C., but was a disaster. The Persian **fleet** was wrecked in a major storm off the Aegean coast in northern Greece. In 490 B.C. Darius and his Persian troops tried again and sailed instead across the Aegean Sea. On their way to take Athens, they first besieged and captured Eretria in Euboea and from there sailed across to the east coast of Attica to the bay of Marathon. The Greeks, with the exception of the Spartans who were busy with a religious festival, went out to meet the Persians at Marathon instead of waiting for them to come to Athens. The first land battle of the Persian Wars followed. This was the Battle of Marathon. Even though the Persians were far more numerous than the Greeks in manpower, Athenian battle tactics allowed for a major Greek victory. The Persian ships that were not captured by the Greeks after the battle proceeded to sail around Attica in order to take Athens while the city was unprotected.

However, the Greeks were quicker and returned to defend Athens by that evening. At this point, the Persians decided to withdraw and return to Asia. Darius's second expedition had failed, and Greek morale was high. The victory at Marathon had shown the Greeks that they could withstand the mighty Persians. The Persians, however, were to return ten years later under the next ruler, King Xerxes.

After the victory at Marathon, Athens began to build up a strong navy in case of another Persian attack. This was accomplished by the great politician of Athens at that time, Themistocles. Two hundred new warships called *triremes* were built. A trireme was a ship of about 120 feet long and 12 feet wide that was powered by three sets of oars. Each trireme had a crew of 170 rowers, a boatswain, a helmsman, 20 marines, and a few officers.

Battle of Thermopylae

In 480 B.C. the Persians returned to fight another war. Xerxes was determined to take revenge on the Greeks and decided to invade. He crossed the **Hellespont** (the narrow strait of water connecting the Sea of Marmara and the Aegean Sea), then both his army and his fleet advanced along the Aegean coast and finally down into Greece. The first battles between the Greeks and the Persians were fought both by land and sea. The sea battle took place at Cape Artemision, north of Euboea. At the same time, a land battle was fought at Thermopylae, a narrow pass between Thessaly and Boeotia that the Persians had to cross to reach Athens. At this battle three hundred Spartans led by King Leonidas met their deaths at the hands of the Persians. The main Greek forces had not arrived in time for the battle. The Spartan soldiers put up a noble resistance. None tried to retreat but fought till the last man fell, showing the bravery and courage of the Spartan soldier. This battle is considered the most "glorious" defeat in Greek history. After the Persian victory at Thermopylae, the Persian forces were now in control of central Greece and were on the way to occupying and destroying Athens.

Monument to the Spartans at Thermopylae

Battle of Salamis

Meanwhile in Athens, Themistocles persuaded most of the Athenians to evacuate the city and assemble the Athenian fleet at Salamis, an island off the coast of Athens. The Delphic **oracle** (a priestess located in the sanctuary of Apollo in Delphi where the Greeks could get advice from the gods on any matter they wished, with the answers given in the form of riddles) had told Themistocles that Athens would be saved by "wooden walls," which he took to mean a wall of ships. When the Persians found the city of Athens deserted, they set fire to it and destroyed it. They soon were tricked by Themistocles into fighting the Athenians in the bay of Salamis. The Battle of Salamis was chaotic and bloody. "The sea was full of wreckage and blood. . . . never in one day did such a multitude of men die." (Herodotus, VII, 420ff.) At the end, the Athenians were victorious and Xerxes ordered his Persian troops to withdraw. He himself went back to Persia, but left behind a Persian land force in northern Greece. A year later in 479 B.C., the Greek army attacked and defeated the remaining Persian army at the Battle of Plataea, in Boeotia. The Persians were forced to withdraw back to Persia. The last action of the Persian Wars, supposedly fought on the same day as the Battle of Plataea, was a sea battle at Cape Mycale in Ionia, where the remainder of the Persian fleet was destroyed. The war was finished. The Greeks were victorious in driving the Persians out of Greece. They had liberated their land from the barbarians.

Name: _____   Date: _____

Knowledge Check

Matching

_____   1. Royal Road
_____   2. fleet
_____   3. Persians
_____   4. oracle
_____   5. trireme
_____   6. satrapies
_____   7. Ionian Revolt
_____   8. Hellespont

a. a group of ships

b. provinces in the Persian empire

c. narrow strait of water connecting the Sea of Marmara and the Aegean Sea

d. people who occupied the area east of the Tigris River in western Asia

e. Greek ship powered by three sets of oars

f. Greeks living in Asia Minor decided to revolt against their foreign rulers

g. priestess who would deliver advice from the gods in the form of a riddle

h. ran from the capital city of Sousa to Sardis

Multiple Choice

9. Who was the king of Persia during the Ionian Revolt?

a. Cyrus
c. Darius

b. Cambyses
d. Xerxes

10. What destroyed the Persian fleet during the first expedition to invade mainland Greece?

a. a storm
c. the Athenians

b. an earthquake
d. the Spartans

Constructed Response

11. Why were the Greeks able to defeat the Persians despite being outnumbered? Use details from the reading selection to support your answer.

_____

_____

_____

_____

_____

_____

14

The Peloponnesian War and Its Aftermath

Pericles

War Between Athens and Sparta

The remainder of the fifth century B.C. was dominated by another great war. It was a war between the two biggest powers of Greece: Athens and Sparta. The growth and collapse of Athenian seapower was the focus of this period in Greek history, which was reported by the second great Greek historian of the fifth century B.C., Thucydides.

The Delian League

The Persian Wars gave the Greeks pride and a new self-confidence that led to great achievements in the following years. After the war, Athens became the leading Greek city-state. It began in 478 B.C. when she set up a league of Asiatic Greek city-states called the **Delian League**. It protected Ionia and the rest of Greece against any further attack from the Persians. Athens acquired the league's leadership and the cities within the league were obliged to contribute either money or ships. The purpose of the league was to take revenge on the Persians for the sufferings they had caused and liberate all Asiatic and other Greek cities still under Persian control. By 468 B.C. all Greek cities along the Aegean coast were liberated and the Persian fleet was demolished. However, when the mission of the league was accomplished, Athens did not renounce the Delian League. Instead she began forcing the liberated Greek cities to stay in the league under her control. In addition, Athens forced other cities to join the league. Athens thus became the leader of an Athenian sea empire and the greatest power in Greece.

It was the Athenian leader Pericles (461–429 B.C.) who was responsible for Athens' growth in power. He also made Athens the cultural center of Greece. A building program was begun that included the **Parthenon** on the Acropolis, a temple dedicated to the city's patron goddess Athena. He also connected Athens and its port, Piraeus, by long walls to protect the city against attacks. With his ambitious political policy, he was responsible for bringing Athens into a war against Sparta.

The Peloponnesian League

In the 500s B.C., Sparta had earlier established her own league, called the **Peloponnesian League**, which consisted mostly of cities in the Peloponnese. It was a loose organization of cities that strengthened to oppose Athens. According to Thucidydes, it was Sparta's fear of Athenian power that made war between the two city-states inevitable. This war, called the **Peloponnesian War**, broke out in 431 B.C. and continued for 27 years with a short break between 421 and 415 B.C. The whole of Greece was involved in the war. Athens and her allies (the Delian League) fought on one side of the war and Sparta and her allies (the Peloponnesian League) on the other. (See map on page 18.)

During the first part of the war (431–421 B.C.), Sparta continually ravaged the countryside of Attica, but it had little effect on Athens. No decisive victory on either side was achieved during those ten years. However, **plagues** hit Athens twice during this time and killed a third of her population. One of the victims was Pericles. This was a critical turning point in Athens' destiny. Having lost one of her greatest generals and most experienced politicians, Athens gradually lost control over her sea empire.

Sparta Defeats Athens

A truce was concluded between the two powers in 421 B.C., but war broke out again in 415 B.C. and lasted until 404 B.C. It began when both Athens and Sparta and their allies became involved in a war between some of the Greek city-states in Sicily. Athens sent out a big expedition and after two years of fighting, met with the greatest defeat in Athenian history. She not only lost many men, but also her whole fleet. This incident made Athens' final defeat unavoidable. During the last years of the war, despite some successes in battle, Athens' power diminished. Many of her allies revolted. Her **treasury** was empty of funds needed for the war. An oligarchic revolution in 411 B.C. brought about internal problems. Finally, Sparta received monetary help from the Persians to insure victory. In 405 B.C. a decisive battle near the Hellespont, the Battle of Aegospotami, insured victory for the Spartans. The Athenians surrendered a year later. They had lost the war and their once-mighty sea empire. Peace was declared, and Sparta set up an oligarchic rule in Athens called the **Rule of the Thirty** or Thirty Tyrants. This rule did not last very long, and democracy was restored in Athens in 403 B.C. After the defeat of Athens in the Peloponnesian War, Sparta now became the leading power in Greece, taking over the empire once ruled by Athens.

Fighting Among the City-States

At this point in Greek history, the Greek historian Xenophon takes over the account of Greece during the fourth century B.C. The fourth century is characterized by the rivalry between various Greek city-states, most prominently Sparta, Athens, and Thebes in various alliances. This conflict between the city-states eventually weakened the Greeks and led to the takeover of Greece by the King of Macedon, Philip II, in 338 B.C.

Between 395 and 386 B.C., Athens, in alliance with Thebes and other city-states with the support of Persia, was involved in a war to put down Sparta's growing power. Peace was subsequently imposed temporarily in 386 B.C. by the King of Persia. This was called the **King's Peace**. The terms included the abandonment of all Asiatic Greek city-states back to Persia. The peace did allow Sparta to continue its dominant power in Greece; however, Sparta's arrogance led to more fighting, and finally, her power was destroyed at the Battle of Leuctra in 371 B.C. by the Thebans.

Thebes was under the rule of a very skilled general named Epaminondas, who made his city the center of power in Greece for a short time. However, in 362 B.C. the allied forces of Sparta and Athens fought against Thebes at the Battle of Mantinea, and even though the Thebans won the battle, Epaminondas was killed. Since there was no one to replace his excellent leadership, Thebes' brief period of dominance came to an end. Fighting among various city-states continued until 338 B.C., and no one city-state was stronger than another.

The Rise of Macedonia

In the meantime another state in the north, Macedonia, was rising to power under its king, Philip II. In 359 B.C. he united the Macedonian state and built up a loyal and professional army, which brought him great successes in battle. While the Greek city-states were quarreling among themselves, Philip extended his influence over the whole of Greece. Except for one man, the orator Demosthenes, no one in Athens foresaw Philip's actions of conquest. Philip eventually conquered the Greeks in 338 B.C. at the Battle of Chaeronea. By then the Greeks were too weak and disorganized to stand up to him.

Name: _____ Date: _____

Knowledge Check

Matching

_____ 1. Delian League

_____ 2. Peloponnesian League

_____ 3. Parthenon

_____ 4. plague

_____ 5. treasury

_____ 6. Peloponnesian War

_____ 7. Rule of the Thirty

_____ 8. King's Peace

a. an outbreak of contagious disease

b. temple dedicated to Athens' patron goddess Athena

c. organization of city-states led by Sparta

d. organization of city-states led by Athens

e. period when Sparta ruled Athens with a group of thirty tyrants

f. war between Athens and Sparta that lasted 27 years

g. the King of Persia imposed a temporary peace among the Greek city-states

h. the money a nation has to carry out its operations

Multiple Choice

9. Why was the Delian League originally formed?

    a. to raise money for Athens

    b. to attack Sparta

    c. to control all Greek city-states

    d. to protect Ionia from the Persians

10. What city-state led by Philip II was able to conquer the whole of Greece?

    a. Thebes

    b. Macedonia

    c. Athens

    d. Sparta

Constructed Response

11. What were the reasons for Athens' defeat in the Peloponnesian War? Use details from the reading selection to support your answer.

_____

_____

_____

_____

_____

_____

_____

Name: _____ Date: _____

Map Follow-Up

Directions: Using the map below and details from your reading, explain why cities such as Athens, Sparta, and Thebes developed their own city-states. Give some examples of how the cities were different from each other.

_____

_____

_____

_____

Ancient Greece

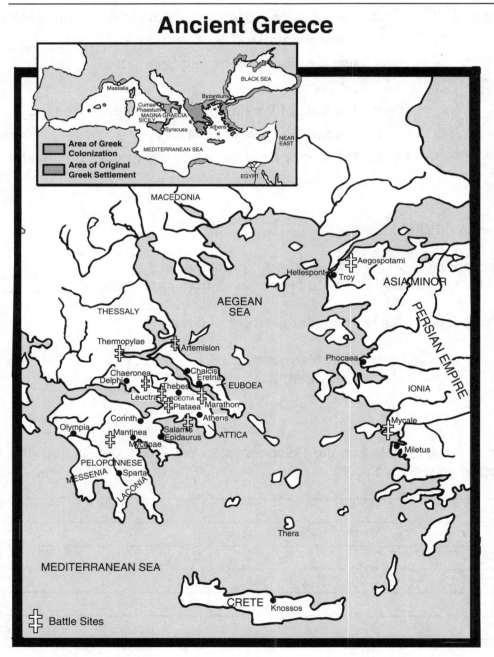

Alexander the Great

Alexander Takes Over in Macedonia

After his conquest of Greece, Philip II of Macedon intended to conquer the Persians and their empire. He died in 336 B.C., however, before he was able to carry out his plan. His son, Alexander, later called "the Great," took over this task and was successful. His achievements are told by the contemporary historian Arrian in his *Anabasis*.

Conquering the Persian Empire

Alexander was 20 years old when he came to the throne of Macedon. He was a very ambitious man and a great general like his father. Just two years later he set out to conquer the Persian Empire, which was ruled by **King Darius III**. With an army of about 35,000 men, he entered Asia Minor and moved south through Syria, Palestine, and Egypt, defeating the Persians in battle at the Granikos River in 334 B.C. and the Issos River in the following year. He occupied Egypt in 332 B.C. where he spent the winter.

Alexander conquered an empire that stretched from Macedonia to Egypt to the Indus River, but he was unable to enjoy the fruits of his labors as he died at the age of 32.

In 331 Alexander marched further inland to the Tigris River. At Gaugamela that same year, he had a decisive victory over Darius III in battle. Alexander was now "King of the Greeks and the Persians." Over the next three years, the king continued his march south and then proceeded eastward toward the **Indus River**, subduing the eastern part of the Persian Empire. He passed through the cities of Babylon, Sousa, Persepolis, and Ecbatana. (See map on page 21.)

Alexander Forced to Turn Back

In 327 B.C. Alexander planned to invade India and crossed the Indus River a year later, but his army was getting tired from the long expedition and all the fighting on the way, so they revolted against him. Alexander was forced to turn back toward Macedonia in 325 B.C. On his way back in 323, while staying in Babylon, Alexander died at the young age of 32. During his campaign into Asia, he had suffered many wounds and sicknesses, and it is said that his weakness made him vulnerable to **malaria**. Others say that he was poisoned.

Spread of Greek Culture

Alexander the Great was indeed a great ruler. His dream was to unify East and West, which he succeeded in doing. He ruled his empire well. He included Greeks and Persians in his administration. Most importantly, Greek culture was spread far and wide throughout the East. Many Greeks settled in Persia, and the cities were organized along Greek lines. He also founded many cities along the way, all called Alexandria. The finest city was the **Alexandria** located on the mouth of the Nile Delta in Egypt. It became the most important trading port in the Mediterranean. A variety of goods from as far away as India passed through this port. Hence, the **Hellenistic civilization** (336–30 B.C.) was created and lasted until the Romans conquered the whole area. **Alexander the Great** was one of the most influential and powerful figures in history and is regarded as one of the greatest conquerors in world history. He left behind a legacy that influenced Roman civilization and, subsequently, the Byzantine Empire.

Name: _____ Date: _____

Knowledge Check

Matching

_____ 1. Alexander the Great

_____ 2. King Darius III

_____ 3. *Anabasis*

_____ 4. malaria

_____ 5. Alexandria

_____ 6. Indus River

_____ 7. Hellenistic civilization

a. finest of the cities named for Alexander, located on the Nile Delta in Egypt

b. ruler of the Perisan empire during this time

c. culture influenced by the Greeks from 336–30 B.C.

d. one of the most powerful figures and greatest conquerors in world history

e. disease that includes fever and chills that is spread by mosquitoes

f. river in present-day Pakistan that marked the eastern edge of Alexander's conquest

g. history written by Arrian that told of Alexander's achievements

Multiple Choice

8. In which battle did Alexander decisively defeat Darius III?

   a. Babylon
   c. Issos River

   b. Alexandria
   d. Gaugamela

9. How far east did Alexander's conquests take him?

   a. across the Tigris River
   c. to the Granikos River

   b. across the Indus River
   d. to the Issos River

Critical Thinking

10. Do you think Alexander deserved the title "the Great"? Why or why not? Use details from the reading selection to support your answer.

_____

_____

_____

_____

_____

_____

Name: _____   Date: _____

Map Follow-Up

Directions: Using the map below and an atlas, work out which modern countries were wholly or partly within the area of Alexander's empire.

_____

_____

_____

_____

_____

_____

Alexander's Empire 336–323 B.C.

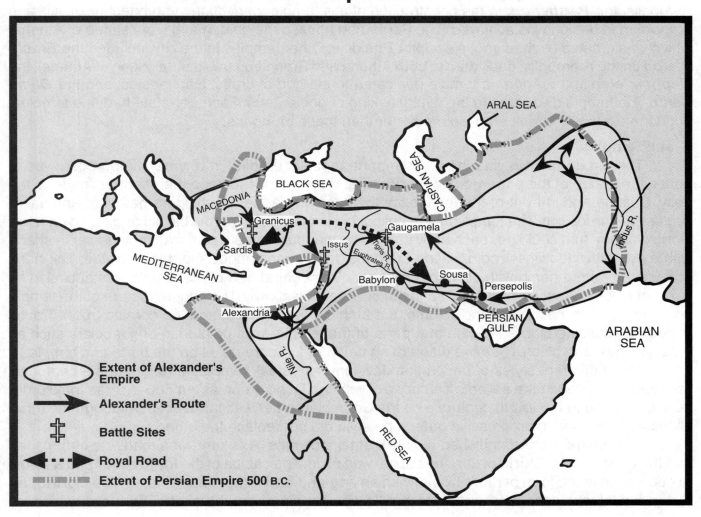

Greek Art and Architecture

The Architecture of Athens

Athens was considered the cultural center of ancient Greece. The city best exemplifies the typical **architecture** to be seen in a Greek city-state.

Towering above the city of Athens stood the **Acropolis,** the sacred hill dedicated to the city's patron-goddess, Athena. Below the Acropolis lay the **Agora,** the commercial and political center of the city. During the fifth century B.C. at the peak of Athens' political power, Pericles initiated the construction of

The Acropolis was the sacred hill in Athens where the Parthenon (top right) and other temples stood.

many public buildings to replace the ones destroyed during the Persian Wars. These monuments still stand today and are admired by many tourists who visit Greece.

Among the most impressive buildings is the temple dedicated to Athena Parthenos on the Acropolis, the **Parthenon**. In the construction of this temple, perfection in both technical skill and proportion in design was achieved. The Parthenon housed the golden and ivory statue of Athena, which was created by the famous sculptor Pheidias. Other temples in the city included the **Erechtheion** on the Acropolis, dedicated to both Athena and Erechteus (a legendary king of Athens); the **Hephaisteion** in the Agora, a temple dedicated to the god of crafts, Hephaestus; and the **Olympeion,** the temple dedicated to the almighty king of gods, Zeus. Each city-state had fine temples, but none exemplify Greek architecture better than those of Athens.

Greek Temples

The Greek **temple** was the most important public building in any city. Its purpose was to house the statue of the patron-god or goddess and sometimes to keep the offerings made to the deity. Outside and in front of the temple lay the altar where the worshippers gathered and sacrifices were carried out. The temples were built of big limestone or marble blocks and stood on a low stone platform that could be reached by steps. The standard temple plan was rectangular in shape with a central windowless room, called the *naos.* In this room stood the deity's statue. The naos opened out onto a porch with columns (*pronaos*). The central part of the temple was encircled by a row of columns that formed the *colonnade* or covered walkway. The superstructure of the temple consisted of four main parts: the column, the architrave, the frieze, and the cornice (roof). Traces of color on building blocks indicate that parts of the temple were painted in bright colors such as reds, yellows, and blues. (See the diagram on page 24 for more detail on the parts of a temple.)

Three different styles of decoration developed in Greek temples throughout the centuries. Temples originated in the seventh century B.C. with the Doric order. About 500 B.C. the Ionic order developed, and in the fourth century B.C., the Corinthian order was introduced. Although the three styles were created in progressive order, one style did not replace the other.

The orders are distinguished mainly by their columns. A column was made up of the shaft and the capital. In the **Doric order**, the capital was plain. The capital of the **Ionic order** had a *volute* (a decoration in the form of ram's horns) with an egg-and-dart pattern underneath. The **Corinthian order** capital was decorated with acanthus leaves growing from the shaft. The frieze, which lay between the cornice and the architrave, was decorated with stone carvings. In the Doric order, it was divided into panels (*metopes*) separated by three vertical grooves (*triglyphs*), while in the Ionic order, the frieze was decorated with a continuous strip. Whereas the architrave was plain in the Doric order, in the Ionic order, it was divided into three equally wide horizontal sections. The Corinthian order had only the capital as its distinguishing feature. The rest of the superstructure was taken over from the Ionic order. The roof of the temple, known as the cornice, was triangular in shape. It consisted of the pediment and the geison, which are the outer edges of the roof. The pediment was always filled with sculptures that represented stories related to the temple's deity, such as the birth of Athena on the Parthenon. The sculptures were brightly painted like the building parts of the temple itself. The three Greek architectural styles, especially the columns, have often been copied in the architecture of subsequent periods and in modern times.

Sculpture

The Greeks were not only great architects but also great sculptors. As already mentioned above, the temples were decorated with sculpted carvings, and a statue of the deity stood inside the building. One famous **sculptor**, mentioned earlier, was Pheidias, who made the statue of Athena entirely out of gold and ivory. Nothing of this statue remains, but descriptions exist in literature and from Roman copies. Most temple statues, however, were made of marble or bronze. Female and male statues of gods, heroes, and Olympic victors (mostly nude) also decorated many of the houses and public buildings or lined the streets. The statues were life-sized figures sculpted either from marble or cast in bronze. Detail was stressed and natural movement and appearance were emphasized. Many of the original statues have not survived, because they were either broken or, in the case of bronze, melted and reused. However, Roman copies have survived, and they provide valuable information about the original Greek works.

Reproduction of Pheidias' Statue of Athena

Pottery

Pottery was another important form of Greek art. It was widely traded throughout the Mediterranean. It came in a variety of shapes depending on the practical purpose. Pottery was used to transport perishable goods such as wine, olive oil, grain, or perfume. It was also used in domestic activities such as cooking and eating, or in religious ceremonies to carry offerings to the gods and as offerings in temples and tombs. Sometimes it was made and traded solely for its artistic merit. Pottery provides useful information for the historian, because many of the vases were painted with scenes of daily life, athletic activities, religious ceremonies, or mythological subjects. Like all forms of Greek art and architecture, Greek pottery production reached its height during the fifth century B.C. Two popular types of pottery were produced: Black Figure and Red Figure pottery. The clay used to make the pottery was fired red in color, due to its high iron content. In **Black Figure pottery**, the figures were drawn in black on the red background. In **Red Figure pottery**, the reverse was true. The figures, outlined in black, were left red on a black-glazed background. Writing was common on pots either to mark the potter's name, to indicate names of mythological or historical figures shown, or to describe the subject matter.

Today, Greek architecture, sculpture, and pottery are highly valued as historical evidence and as skilled works of art.

Architectural Orders and Parts of a Greek Temple

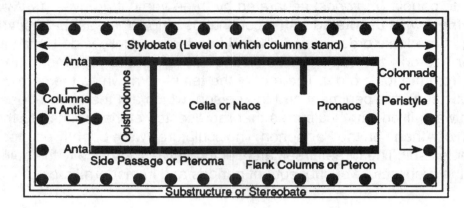

Stylobate (Level on which columns stand)

Anta

Columns in Antis

Opisthodomos

Cella or Naos

Pronaos

Colonnade or Peristyle

Anta

Side Passage or Pteroma

Flank Columns or Pteron

Substructure or Stereobate

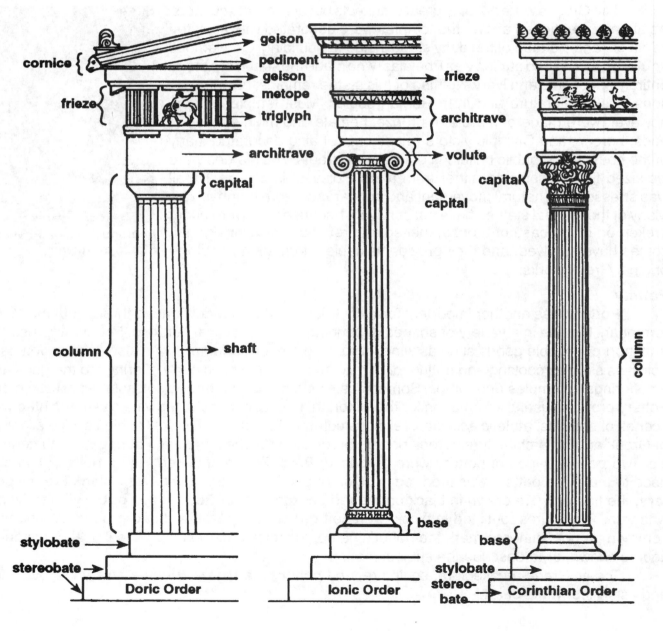

cornice

geison

pediment

geison

metope

frieze

triglyph

architrave

capital

column

shaft

stylobate

stereobate

Doric Order

frieze

architrave

volute

capital

base

Ionic Order

capital

column

base

stylobate

stereo-bate

Corinthian Order

Name: _____ Date: _____

Knowledge Check

Matching

_____ 1. Acropolis

_____ 2. Agora

_____ 3. temple

_____ 4. Ionic order

_____ 5. Doric order

_____ 6. Corinthian order

_____ 7. sculpture

_____ 8. architecture

_____ 9. pottery

a. artform that uses clay to make pots, vases, etc., used to store and serve items and as art objects

b. the art or science of designing and building structures

c. the process of carving or forming hard materials to produce a three-dimensional work of art

d. the commercial and political center of Athens

e. the sacred hill in Athens dedicated to Athena

f. featured a capital with ram's horns and egg-and-dart pattern

g. featured a plain capital

h. featured a capital with acanthus leaves

i. building that housed the statue of the patron-god or goddess and sometimes kept the offering made to that diety

Multiple Choice

10. The Olympeion was a temple dedicated to what Greek god?

    a. Athena   b. Erechteus
    c. Hephaestus   d. Zeus

11. Which type of pottery had the figures outlined in black and left red on a black-glazed background?

    a. Black Figure pottery   b. Red Figure pottery
    c. Red Line pottery   d. Black Background pottery

Constructed Response

12. Was a Greek temple like a cathedral or church either in appearance or in the way it was used? Use details from the reading selection to support your answer.

_____

_____

_____

_____

_____

_____

Name: _____   Date: _____

Explore: Identifying the Parts of a Greek Temple

Directions: Identify the architectural orders and the different parts of a Greek temple. Write in the correct terms on the lines next to the parts or make a numbered list on a sheet of paper.

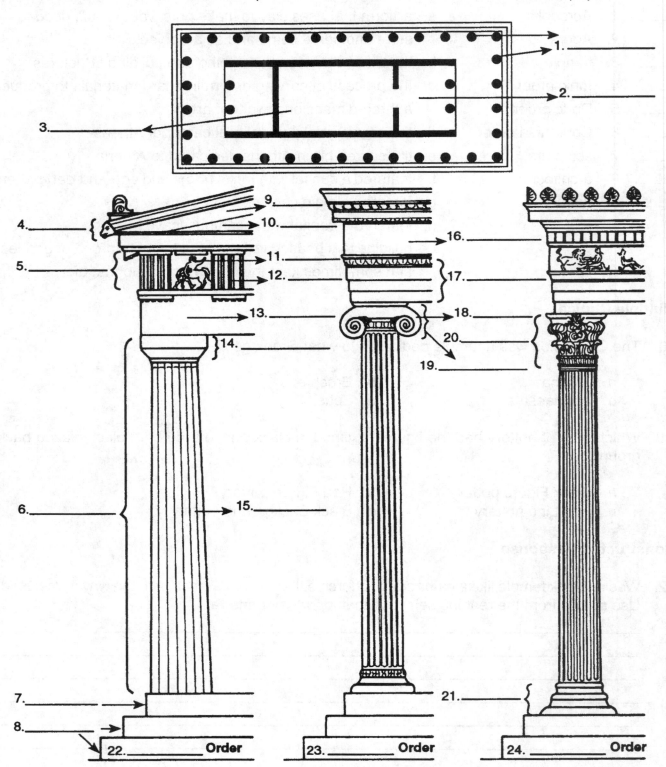

Greek Theater and Games

Greek Theater

Festivals

Each year the Greeks looked forward to being entertained at several festivals held in honor of the gods. The **festivals** were mainly religious events. A festival consisted partially of a procession and sacrifices to the god being honored. It was also a social occasion for the Greeks to get together and enjoy the excitement of plays and athletic events.

The main social event of some of the festivals was the dramatic competition. Examples of such festivals in Athens include the festival of the City Dionysia, held in honor of Dionysus (god of wine and drama), and the Great Panathenaic Festival, held in honor of the city's patron-goddess, Athena.

Drama

Drama, an important contribution to Western civilization, was invented by the Greeks. Greek playwrights produced a large number of high-quality plays, some of which have survived in today's literature. The plays were of two kinds: tragedies and comedies. In **tragedies**, the subject matter dealt mostly with mythological stories, although some plays were based on historical events. The themes of the stories consisted of disasters, bloody revenge, or the suffering of the human conscience. The **comedies** dealt with the ridiculing of political or social issues at hand. In a public performance, only three actors played the various characters in a play. Masks were used to distinguish one character from the other, which made it easier for one actor to play several roles. Essential to all the plays was the *chorus*. The chorus was a group of performers who danced and sang at intervals throughout the play, commenting on the events of the play.

Playwrights and Plays

Fifth century Greece produced some of history's finest **playwrights**. They include Aeschylus, Sophocles, and Euripides (the tragedians) and Aristophanes (the comic poet).

One famous Greek tragedy was *Oedipus the King* by Sophocles. It tells of Oedipus, the son of a king, who was told by the Delphic oracle that he would kill his father and marry his mother. The prophesy was fulfilled, and at the end he gouged out his eyes with his mother's (wife's) broach. The play ends with his life in ruins.

One of Aeschylus's surviving plays, *The Persians,* dealt with the historical battle of Salamis in 480 B.C. The battle was described so vividly that he must have been an eyewitness of the event, if not a participant as well.

Aristophanes is famous for his parodies of his rival playwrights, philosophers, and statesmen, as well as for making a mockery of the Athenian democracy. The plots of his plays were outlandish, sometimes involving talking animals. He used vulgar language and made obscene jokes.

The Theater

The building in which the plays were held was the **theater**. The Greek theater was a semi-circular structure, usually built on the slope of a hill. The main feature of a theater was the *orchestra,* the central acting area, which was surrounded three-quarters of the way by the seating area. At the open end of the orchestra stood the stage building or *skene,* where the actors could change and store their belongings. The first theaters were simple structures built on the natural slope of the hill and made of wood. In the fourth century B.C., the structures became permanent and were made of stone. Many of the stone theaters still stand today. The most famous theater is at Epidaurus, in the Peloponnese. It is still used today for the performance of ancient Greek plays.

The Olympic Games

Athletic competitions were the main attractions of other Greek festivals. The most prestigious of these festivals was the **Olympic Games**, held in honor of Zeus, the king of gods. The event took place every four years in the sanctuary of Zeus at Olympia, located in the northwest part of the Peloponnese. The sanctuary of Zeus was a sacred area dedicated to the god and his wife, Hera. After the Olympic Games were instituted in Zeus's honor, the sanctuary grew in size. Not only were temples and altars erected for the religious activities, but a stadium and **hippodrome** (a stadium designed for equestrian events) were constructed for the athletic events. In the beginning, athletes and spectators alike had to live uncomfortably in the open air. Buildings to accommodate the athletes and the spectators were absent until fairly late in the history of the sanctuary. In the fourth century B.C. a guest house, a gymnasium, and two bath houses were built to ease the comfort of the people and competitors. The Olympic Games first originated in 776 B.C. The Games continue in a modern form today. Like all festivals, religious observances were a main part of the ceremony, which included sacrifices made to the honored god.

There were eight different types of athletic competitions that took place over a three-day period at the Olympic Games. The chariot races and the horse races were carried out in the hippodrome. The chariots had two wheels and were pulled by four horses. Crashes and fatalities were frequent during the chariot races. The remainder of the athletic events took place in the stadium. The stadium was about 200 meters long (600 feet) with the natural slopes of a hill serving as the seating area for the spectators and the judges. The events consisted of boxing, wrestling, the *pankration* (a mix of boxing, wrestling, and judo), track events, a race in armor, and the *pentathlon*. The pentathlon was a five-part contest that included the discus throw, the long jump, the javelin throw, a 200-meter run, and wrestling. The track events consisted of three running races: the 200 meter, the 400 meter, and a longer race of about 5,000 meters. The race in armor was the final athletic competition and demonstrates the importance of the **hoplite** (a type of heavily armed soldier) in the Greek army.

Olympic athletes competed in eight different types of competition.

There was only one winner for every contest. There were no second- and third-place winners. The winners of the various contests were rewarded with simple garlands of olive leaves, but the prestige associated with being an Olympic victor was great. At home, the victor might get some money prizes or free meals for the rest of his life. Sometimes statues of the victors were sculpted and displayed in public places. The victors were seen as heroes.

Other games were established in Greece, but none were as prestigious as the Olympic Games. Two of these were the Pythian Games at Delphi, held every four years, and the Isthmian Games at Corinth, held every two years.

Many Greeks from faraway places flocked to see the festivals. They were very religious people who did not want to anger the gods by not attending the festivals. At the same time, the festivals were social events that were not to be missed.

Name: _____ Date: _____

Knowledge Check

Matching

_____ 1. drama

_____ 2. festivals

_____ 3. comedies

_____ 4. tragedies

_____ 5. chorus

_____ 6. theater

_____ 7. Olympic Games

_____ 8. hippodrome

_____ 9. hoplite

a. made fun of political or social issues at hand

b. group of performers who danced and sang at intervals throughout the play

c. telling a story through actors and dialogue

d. dealt with myths and historical events

e. a heavily armed Greek soldier

f. consisted of a procession and sacrifices to the god being honored; also a social occasion

g. a stadium designed for equestrian (horse) events

i. athletic competition held every four years in honor of Zeus

j. a semi-circular structure, usually built on the slope of a hill, with the orchestra area for acting and the skene where the actors could change

Multiple Choice

10. Which of the following playwrights wrote comedies?

    a. Euripides

    c. Sophocles

    b. Aristophanes

    d. Aeschylus

11. Which of the Olympic events featured a five-part contest?

    a. pentathlon

    c. pankration

    b. chariot races

    d. race in armor

Tragedy and Comedy Masks

Constructed Response

12. What are some differences between the Greek Olympic Games and the modern ones? Use details from the reading selection and what you know about the modern Olympics to support your answer.

_____

_____

_____

_____

_____

_____

The Etruscans and the Beginnings of Rome

Etruscan Couple Carved on a Sarcophagus

Early Settlers of Italy

The peninsula of Italy was centrally located in the Mediterranean Sea and became the home of many peoples. It had fertile soil for cultivation as well as a pleasant climate and a variety of metal ores, such as copper and iron. Indo-European people migrated to Italy from the north in two successive waves. First, in about 2000 B.C. people who used bronze tools and weapons arrived. Then, about 1000 B.C., Iron Age people moved in, using superior iron tools and weapons. These were the ancestors of the different Italic tribes that inhabited most of Italy by the ninth century B.C. Most notable of the Italic tribes were the **Latins** who lived near Rome in the area called Latium. Between 750 and 600 B.C. the **Greeks** settled to the south of Rome in the area known as Magna Graecia. To the north of Rome, between the Tiber and Arno Rivers, the **Etruscans** settled in the area known as Etruria. (See map on page 36.)

The Etruscans

The Etruscans were self-governed and lived in this region from the eighth century B.C. until they were conquered by the Romans in the third century B.C. It is not known where the Etruscans came from. Some historians claim they migrated from Asia, while others claim they were native to Italy. It is known that they were not Indo-European, and they spoke an unknown language. The Etruscans have left behind numerous monuments and artifacts that attest to an advanced and flourishing civilization in pre-Roman Italy.

The Etruscans were organized into a confederation of twelve city-states, each with its own king. Some examples were Caere, Tarquinia, Chuisi, Populonia, Veii, and Volsinii. Volsinii was the religious center, and a religious festival was held there annually. The city-states were built on low hilltops surrounded by strong fortifications. An extensive road system connected the city-states.

The Etruscans were skilled bronze workers. They made bronze pots, tools, weapons, sculptures, and household items. In their artwork, they were greatly influenced by the Greeks in the south, who traded extensively with them. They also adopted the Greek alphabet to write their language and in turn passed it on to the Romans, who used it to write Latin.

Extensive *necropoli* (cemeteries) scattered the landscape. The Etruscans buried their dead in monumental tombs. These tombs consisted of rock-cut chambers that were often covered by a large *tumulus* (mound of earth). The local rock was called **tufa**, a rock of volcanic origin that was very soft and easily cut. The Etruscans cut family tombs in the tufa cliffs that looked like the insides of their houses, with several chambers connected to a main chamber. On stone benches inside the chambers lay carved *sarcophagi* (stone caskets) in which the dead were laid to rest. In tombs found at Tarquinia, paintings with scenes of everyday life decorate the tombs and give valuable information to archaeologists. When the Etruscans were conquered by the Romans, they started cremating their dead and putting the ashes in carved stone urns. On many sarcophagi and urns, portraits of the dead were sculpted in stone, and a carving of the dead person's name, family, and occupation was inscribed.

The Etruscans were at their height of power between the seventh and fifth centuries B.C. They expanded their territory beyond their homeland of Etruria to the north as far as Bologna and to the south into Campania. This included the settlement of Rome on the Tiber River. Rome was an aggregate of separate villages that had been united into one community by the mid-eighth century B.C. The inhabitants of Rome, who were Latins, lived in primitive huts made of thatch and mud. During the time of the Etruscan occupation, Rome grew into a city and flourished. A century later Rome took the lead and began, little by little, to take over all the peoples of Italy: the Italic tribes, the Greeks, and the Etruscans.

The Romans

According to legend, Rome was founded by the twins **Romulus** and **Remus** in 753 B.C. Titius Livius (known as Livy) describes the events of the early history of Rome and its foundation. He tells how after the sack of Troy by the Greeks, a Trojan prince, Aeneas, sailed around the Mediterranean and eventually landed in Italy, where he settled. Aeneas married the daughter of King Latinus, the king of the Latins. After Aeneas' son founded a new city, Alba Longa (near Rome), he and his descendants ruled the city for thirteen generations until Amulius seized the throne from the real king, Numitor. Numitor had twin grandchildren, Romulus and Remus, whom a servant, on Amulius's orders, was supposed to

This bronze wolf is thought to have been made by an Etruscan artist in about 500 B.C.

drown in the Tiber River. Instead, the servant left the twins in a basket on the river bank. A she-wolf nursed them until a shepherd found and raised them. When the boys reached manhood, they took revenge upon Amulius and killed him. Together they founded a new city on the spot where they had been left behind as babies. After a quarrel, however, Romulus killed his brother and became the first king of the newly-founded city, which was named Rome after him. A bronze she-wolf from about 500 B.C., a masterpiece made by an Etruscan artist, can still be seen in Rome today.

The Monarchy

Romulus was followed by six more kings. The fifth and seventh kings of Rome were Etruscan in origin. With the fifth king, Tarquinius Priscus, the period in which the Etruscans dominated Rome and the Latins began. During that time, Rome became a city surrounded by a defensive wall with a central marketplace (the **Forum**), public buildings, and temples. When Etruscan power began to decline in Latium and Campania during the sixth century B.C., the last king, Tarquinius Superbus, was expelled by the Roman aristocrats. The traditional date for the end of this period known as the **"Monarchy,"** which began in 753 with the founding of Rome, is 509 B.C. This date (509 B.C.) also marks the beginning of Roman civilization.

The Etruscans are an important part of Roman history because the Romans adopted many customs from them. Examples include the arch and the layout of the temple in Roman architecture, the Etruscan alphabet (adopted from the Greeks) used to write Latin, the reading of the future by looking at the entrails of animals, the art of bronze making, and very importantly, some aspects of Roman government. The Romans were also influenced greatly by the Greek culture, which can be seen in their architecture, sculpture, science, and literature.

Name: _____ Date: _____

Knowledge Check

Matching

_____ 1. Romulus

_____ 2. Remus

_____ 3. Etruscans

_____ 4. necropoli

_____ 5. tumulus

_____ 6. tufa

_____ 7. sarcophagi

_____ 8. Forum

_____ 9. Monarchy

a. group that settled between the Tiber and Arno Rivers and had a confederation of 12 city-states

b. stone caskets

c. a volcanic rock that was soft and easy to cut

d. founder of Rome who killed his brother and became the first king of Rome

e. mound of earth

f. founder of Rome who was killed by his brother

g. central marketplace of Rome

h. cemeteries

i. period from 753 to 509 B.C. when Rome was ruled by kings

Multiple Choice

10. Members of which Italic tribe founded Rome and eventually took over all the people of Italy?

    a. the Greeks   b. the Etruscans
    c. the Indo-Europeans   d. the Latins

11. Etruscans were particulary skilled at working with which metal?

    a. bronze   b. iron
    c. gold   d. steel

Constructed Response

12. To what extent did the Etruscans play a significant role in the development of Rome? Use details from the reading selection to support your answer.

_____

_____

_____

_____

_____

_____

_____

The Republic of Rome
Part 1: 509–218 B.C.

The Republic

With the expulsion of the last king of Rome, a new period in Roman history started, and a new form of government replaced the monarchy. This period is called the **Republic**, a name given to the new state by the Romans.

The king was replaced by two men, called **consuls**, who held all the executive power. They also commanded the army

The Roman Senate

in times of war. They were advised by a governing body of ex-magistrates, known as the **Senate**. This council originated during the Etruscan occupation of the city, when it served as an advisory body to the king. Officially, the responsibility of the Senate remained the same, but as Rome grew in power, it became a very influential body of government in regard to internal and foreign policy. The Senate controlled all matters of great importance, such as decisions of war. Other important positions within the government were the judge of the city **(praetor)**; the financial officer **(quaestor)**; the office of public relations **(aedile)**, which organized festivals and other events; and the high priest **(pontifex maximus)**. The Roman people were divided into two social classes: the **patricians**, who were the land-owning aristocracy, and the **plebeians** or the common people, who were farmers and traders. In the beginning, only the patricians could hold the offices of consul and be members of the Senate, so they controlled the government. It was also a Roman custom that the patricians become the protectors, or **patroni**, of some poorer people, ex-slaves, or newcomers to the city, who were known as **clientes**. The patroni helped the clientes financially and legally in return for help in their political and private lives. This custom of patron-client relationship helped the leading aristocratic families retain their influence in the state, both politically and socially.

The Early Republic

Internally, during the Early Republic phase (509–133 B.C.), discontentment occurred among the plebeians because they were not allowed to participate in the government, and the little land they owned was slowly being taken by the patricians. This left the plebians in a state of debt and servitude, which led to a social struggle between the two classes lasting over 200 years. It was a bloodless revolution, however. By means of strikes and refusing to perform their duties to the state, they sought social and political equality. Little by little the plebeians were given certain rights. Every year elections were held for two men, called "tribunes of the people" (known as **tribuni plebis**), who would represent the people in government affairs. The laws of Rome were published on twelve stone tablets and displayed in the Forum. Gradually plebeians were allowed to enter positions in the government. Finally, a law was passed in 287 B.C. known as the **Lex Hortensia**, in which a People's Assembly was officially recognized. This plebeian assembly had the force of the law. It could pass or veto any law that was put before it and make decisions on matters of the state. In theory, the people had the power, but in practice, it was the Senate who decided the complex and significant matters of the state. This led to more strife between the two classes and eventually to civil war during the second phase of the Republic period (133–30 B.C.)

Rome Becomes a World Power

Externally, during the first three centuries of the Republic, Rome grew to be a world power. With an efficient army and notable leaders, Rome expanded her domain throughout Italy and the Mediterranean. (See inset map on page 36.) Until 300 B.C., the Romans fought the neighboring mountain tribes known as the Volsci, the Aequi, and the Sabini. In 390 B.C., Rome drove off the Gauls who had invaded from the north across the Alps and had ravaged and burnt the city of Rome. Over the next century, the Etruscans of the north and the other Latin tribes of Latium were conquered. During the last thirty years of the fourth century, the Samnites were the enemy. The **Samnites**, who dominated Campania, were the toughest Italic tribe the Romans had to face, but in a series of three wars, the Samnites were finally defeated. By 280 B.C., Rome dominated central and northern

King Pyrrhus of Epirus

Italy. The only people left to conquer in Italy were the Greeks who lived in the south. For fear of a Roman invasion, the Greeks of the city of Tarentum asked for help from their countrymen on the Greek mainland. In 280 B.C., King Pyrrhus of Epirus crossed the Adriatic Sea, landed in Italy, and fought the Romans for five years. The war against the Greeks was called the **Pyrrhic war**, after the Greek king. Pyrrhus was a tough enemy to defeat because he used elephants in his battles against the Romans. At first he was successful, because the Romans had never seen elephants before and were scared. But eventually the Roman army was able to deal with the elephants and defeated Phyrrus in 275 B.C. Pyrrhus withdrew back to Epirus in Greece. By 272 B.C. Tarentum and all the other Greek city-states in Italy had submitted to Rome. Rome made separate alliances with each of the conquered cities. As allies, the cities were independent but had to supply the Romans with men for their army.

The First Punic War

In the third century B.C. the Romans were at war with **Carthage**, the remaining prominent power in the western Mediterranean. Carthage, located on the coast of North Africa, was a colony established by the Phoenicians, a seafaring people from the Syrian coast (present-day Lebanon). The Phoenicians had dominated the western Mediterranean Sea since the ninth century B.C. and had founded many colonies along the Mediterranean coast. Carthage was the most important of these. Within a century, Carthage controlled the North African and Spanish coasts, Sardinia, Corsica, and western Sicily. Rome fought three wars with Carthage. These were called the Punic Wars (Punic is Latin for Phoenician).

The **First Punic War** (264–241 B.C.) broke out because of a conflict of interest over Sicily. Fighting was harsh on both land and sea, but the Roman army was strong. Carthage lost, and a truce was made between the two powers. Rome acquired Sicily and Sardinia, and these islands together became the first province of Rome. A province was controlled by a Roman magistrate, who set up a local government and collected taxes to be paid to Rome. Carthage, however, would not give up. After the First Punic War, the Carthaginians occupied Spain to replace the island territories they had lost. Another clash between Carthage and Rome became inevitable in 218 B.C., when a Carthaginian general sought revenge for his country. The provocation was a conflict about the possession of the Spanish town of Saguntum. The Second Punic War is discussed in the next chapter.

Name: _____   Date: _____

Knowledge Check

Matching

_____ 1. Carthage
_____ 2. clientes
_____ 3. patricians
_____ 4. patroni
_____ 5. plebeians
_____ 6. Republic
_____ 7. Samnites
_____ 8. Senate
_____ 9. tribuni plebis

a. wealthy protectors
b. toughest Italic tribe the Romans had to face
c. tribune of the people
d. poorer people, ex-slaves, and those new to the city
e. governing body of ex-magistrates who advised the consuls
f. colony of the Phoenicians located in North Africa
g. the land-owning aristocracy
h. the name given to the new Roman state governed by two consuls and the Senate
i. the common people; farmers and traders

Multiple Choice

10. In which war did the Romans fight the Greeks?

    a. Pyrrhic War   b. Samnite War
    c. Punic War   d. Etruscan War

11. What was the office of the two men who held the executive power of the Roman Republic and commanded the army?

    a. aedile   b. praetor
    c. pontifex maximus   d. consul

Constructed Response

12. What was the reason for the social struggle between the plebeians and the patricians during the Early Republic? Use details from the reading selection to support your answer.

_____

_____

_____

_____

_____

_____

_____

Name: _____   Date: _____

Map Follow-Up

Directions: Using the map below and the reading selection, trace the three different phases of Roman territorial expansion throughout Italy. List the enemies the Romans had to fight during each phase.

_____

_____

_____

_____

_____

Italy and the Roman World 218 B.C.

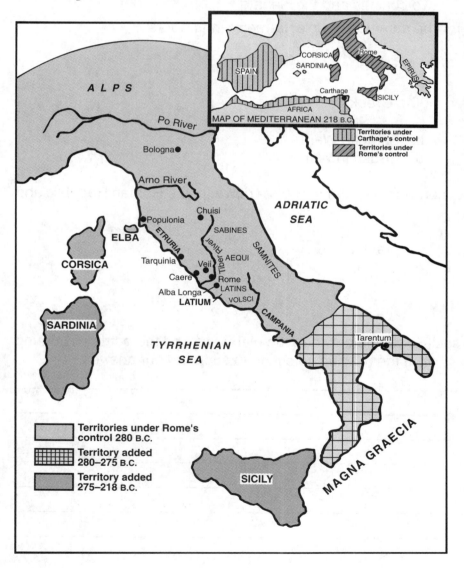

_____

_____

_____

_____

_____

_____

_____

_____

_____

_____

_____

_____

_____

_____

_____

_____

_____

_____

_____

_____

_____

_____

_____

_____

_____

_____

The Republic of Rome Part 2: Hannibal 218–133 B.C.

These coins show Hannibal of Carthage and one of his war elephants.

Hannibal and the Second Punic War

The Carthaginian general who was involved in the events leading up to the **Second Punic War** (218–201 B.C.) was **Hannibal**. He is considered to be one of the ablest and most brilliant generals the Romans ever faced.

Invasion of Rome

Hannibal decided to lead his army, which included elephants, into Italy from the north. (See map on page 39.) He crossed the high, snow-covered **Alps** with difficulty and lost more than half of his elephants and soldiers. Despite his many losses, Hannibal was victorious over the Romans during the first two years of the war. His army forces were not as numerous as those of the Romans, but his generalship and new battle tactics won him a series of battles. The last and greatest victory for Hannibal was at the **Battle of Cannae** in 216 B.C. In this battle, a whole Roman army was destroyed.

Hannibal Crossing the Alps

Scipio

The Romans refused to admit defeat, however. New and more capable generals were chosen to fight the Carthaginians. One such general was **Cornelius Scipio**. While Hannibal remained in Italy waiting for reinforcements to arrive from Spain, an army under Scipio fought the Carthaginian army in Spain. The Romans also prevented Hannibal from receiving any reinforcements by killing his brother in battle. Scipio, adopting Hannibal's battle strategy, drove the Carthaginians out of Spain in 206 B.C.

From Spain, Scipio proceeded to invade Africa and attacked the city of Carthage itself. This move forced Hannibal to leave Italy and meet Scipio in a battle in his home territory. The battle took place in 202 B.C. at **Zama**, where Scipio won a great and final victory over Hannibal. After this victory, Scipio became known as Scipio Africanus, and the defeated Hannibal fled to Asia. A peace agreement between the Carthaginians and the Romans was signed in 201 B.C. Carthaginian might was destroyed, and Spain was made into two Roman **provinces**. The Romans became the leading power of the western Mediterranean.

The Roman Provinces

Rome now focused its attention on the eastern Mediterranean, and her sea empire grew larger. In the first century B.C., she became involved in wars with Macedonia, Greece, and Syria. In 168 B.C. the Kingdom of Macedonia was seized. Greece became part of the Roman Republic in 146 B.C. after a revolt in the city of Corinth was crushed. That same year Carthage was razed to the ground at the end of the Third Punic War. Macedonia and Greece became one Roman province, and Carthage formed the province of Africa. In 133 B.C. King Attalus of Pergamon in Asia died and left his kingdom to the Romans. This became the province of Asia. Hence, by 133 B.C. Rome had established seven provinces on three continents along the Mediterranean: Sicily and Sardinia (one province), Corsica, Spain (two provinces), Africa, Macedonia-Greece, and Asia.

Name: _____   Date: _____

Knowledge Check

Matching

_____ 1. Second Punic War

_____ 2. Hannibal

_____ 3. Alps

_____ 4. Battle of Cannae

_____ 5. Cornelius Scipio

_____ 6. Zama

_____ 7. province

a. battle where Scipio won a final victory over Hannibal

b. battle where Hannibal destroyed a whole Roman army

c. a country or region under the control of the Roman government

d. war between Carthage and Rome from 218 to 201 B.C.

e. brilliant general who led the Carthaginians

f. high, snow-covered mountains in northern Italy

g. Roman general who defeated Hannibal

Multiple Choice

8. After which war did Carthage become a province of Rome?

   a. First Punic War
   c. Third Punic War
   b. Second Punic War
   d. Fourth Punic War

9. How did the Romans get the province of Asia?

   a. They fought three wars with the Phoenicians.
   b. King Attalus of Pergamon died and left his kingdom to the Romans.
   c. Scipio defeated Hannibal at the Battle of Zama.
   d. Rome took over the province of Asia when they defeated the Greeks.

Constructed Response

10. What were the reasons for the eventual and final Roman victory over Carthage and its general, Hannibal? Use details from the reading selection to support your answer.

_____

_____

_____

_____

_____

_____

_____

_____

Name: _____   Date: _____

Map Follow-Up

Directions: Using the map below and the reading selection, trace Roman territorial expansion from the end of the First Punic War to 133 B.C. Name the seven provinces the Romans had acquired.

_____

_____

_____

_____

_____

_____

Expansion of the Roman World 218 B.C.–A.D. 120

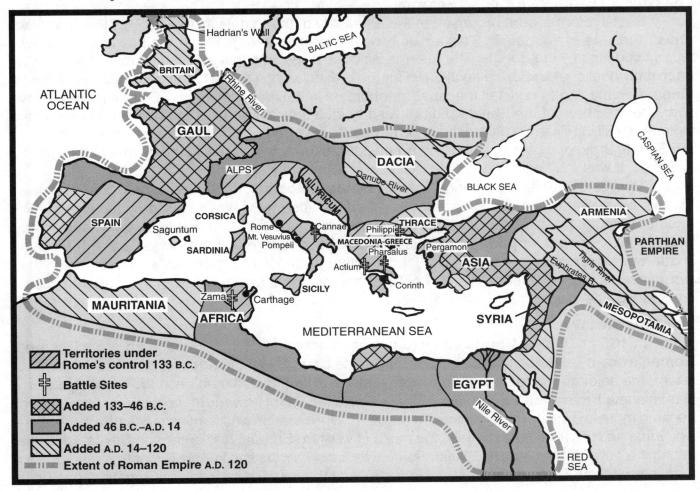

The Republic of Rome Part 3: Civil Wars 133–46 B.C.

Unrest Among the People

The war with Hannibal had harmful effects on the political situation in Rome and Italy. Much of the farmland was left in ruins, having been plundered by Hannibal's troops and abandoned by its owners, who had to serve in the Roman army. As a result, many of the **soldier-farmers** were left without property, became unemployed

Gaius Gracchus Acting as Tribune of the People

and poor, and moved to the big cities. The state bought up the small farms and leased them to the wealthy **upper class**. Farms became larger, and products such as olives and grapes were cultivated on a large scale for commercial purposes. This trend only increased the gap between the rich and the poor. The Senate, which consisted of the wealthy landowners, also remained in full control of the state. The Republic's constitution was not in the hands of the people as designed. This led to unrest among the people. Reforms were needed to prevent anarchy from breaking out.

The Gracchi Brothers Propose Reforms

Social reforms were proposed to the Assembly of the People in 133 B.C. by **Tiberius Gracchus**, a tribune of the people. This action, which was in accordance with the Lex Hortensia, was bitterly opposed by the Senate. The reforms included a law setting a maximum amount of property each individual could hold. It also allowed for the redistribution of land to the poor citizens of Rome. Tiberius was trying to reinstall the small landholders in Italy and take care of urban poverty. However, the members of the Senate did not wish to lose their property or their power. They reacted violently by killing Tiberius before the reforms could be carried out. The assassination of Tiberius by the Senate proved to be damaging and is considered the turning point in the history of the Roman Republic. It was the beginning of the decline and fall of the Republic.

Ten years later, the brother of Tiberius, **Gaius Gracchus**, attempted to pass the same laws that his brother had proposed. His attempt failed because he was also killed by the Senate. For another century, the struggle between the people, who sought more power, and the aristocracy, who fought to keep their power, continued. Each faction was led by men who tried to rebuild the shattered Republican constitution. The leaders were distinguished generals who had proven their worth in wars in Europe and Asia. But political and personal rivalry between the leaders became common. Social disorder and civil wars resulted.

The First Civil War

In 107 B.C. **Gaius Marius** came to power as consul of Rome. He created a **professional Roman army** by allowing the poor citizens from the cities to join the army for terms of 16 years. In return, the soldiers would be rewarded with a piece of land to settle on once their military service was finished. This military reform was instrumental to the rise of powerful generals because the army became more loyal to its generals than to the state. While Marius was fighting the **Gauls**, barbarians who inhabited the area north of Italy and much of western Europe, his lieutenant, **Cornelius Sulla**, became a powerful general. In 88 B.C. Rome was facing a rebellion in Asia Minor that required Roman intervention. The people wanted Marius to lead the war, but instead, the Senate chose Sulla, who had become a consul. As a result, Sulla marched on Rome and declared Marius an outlaw. Marius fled to Africa, and Sulla went to the east to deal with the rebellion. As soon as Sulla left for Asia Minor, however, Marius and his supporters took control of Rome once again. Marius died in 86 B.C., but his followers continued the battle. In 82 B.C., on his way back from the east, Sulla again marched on Rome with his army, and the first civil war broke out. The two forces, Marius' followers supported by the people and Sulla's troops supported by the Senate, met in a battle outside Rome. Sulla was victorious and declared himself dictator of Rome. He was put in charge to restore the old Republican constitution and did so by restoring much of the Senate's power in the government and breaking the power of the people. In 80 B.C. he resigned from his dictatorship; he died the following year.

Pompey and Crassus

The new power of the Senate did not last long. Two brilliant generals, Pompeius Magnus, known as Pompey, and Crassus, became powerful leaders. **Pompey** had increased his military reputation with victorious campaigns in Spain. **Crassus** was put in command of the Roman army to repress a slave rebellion led by a professional gladiator, **Spartacus**, in southern Italy. After two years of fighting, Crassus was able to capture Spartacus with the help of Pompey, who had just returned from Spain. Spartacus was killed, and thousands of his fellow slaves were crucified. Pompey and Crassus decided to run together for the consulship of Rome in 70 B.C.

Pompey

During their consulship, they overturned Sulla's laws and restored the power to the people, thus weakening the power of the Senate. The conflicts between the Senate and the people resumed. While Crassus stayed in Rome, Pompey continued to increase his military reputation in campaigns in the east. He expanded Rome's territories by combining Pontus and Bythinia into the Roman province of Bythinia in 68 B.C. He defeated the last king of the Seleucid Empire in Syria in 63 B.C. and enlarged the province of Asia. Lastly, the kingdom of Judaea in Palestine became a client state of Rome.

The First Triumvirate

While Pompey was in the east, **Gaius Julius Caesar** became popular in Rome through his victories in Spain. Trouble was also brewing in Rome—a conspiracy in 63 B.C. led by Cateline almost overthrew the state. The Senate increasingly insulted Pompey, Crassus, and Caesar, with the result that they joined forces to form a coalition, called the **First Triumvirate** (60–53 B.C.), in which all three men shared the power of the state. The growing ambitions of the leaders, who commanded their own armies, soon led to another civil war, however. Caesar had just finished the conquest of Gaul (58–51 B.C.). Fearing the power of Caesar, Pompey forced him to disarm his troops and accept humiliation before returning to Rome. But Caesar did not wish to give up everything for which he had fought, so he and his army crossed into Italy, starting

Julius Caesar

the second civil war (49–46 B.C.). Due to his brilliant generalship and speed of movement, Caesar won a series of major battles against Pompey's forces, defeating Pompey himself in 48 B.C. at the Battle of Pharsalus in Greece. (See map on page 39.) After defeating Pompey's sons and other Pompeian supporters in Africa and Spain in 46 B.C., Caesar became sole ruler of the Republic and was appointed dictator of Rome for life.

Name: _____ Date: _____

Knowledge Check

Matching

_____ 1. soldier-farmers

_____ 2. upper class

_____ 3. professional Roman army

_____ 4. Gauls

_____ 5. Pompey

_____ 6. Crassus

_____ 7. Spartacus

_____ 8. Gaius Julius Caesar

_____ 9. First Triumvirate

a. a professional gladiator who led a slave rebellion

b. Pompey, Crassus, and Caesar shared power

c. barbarians in the area north of Italy

d. lost their property when they had to fight in the army; became unemployed and poor

e. was appointed dictator of Rome for life

f. general with victories in Spain and Asia

g. shared power with Pompey and Caesar

h. wealthy landowners

i. poor citizens were allowed to join the army for terms of 16 years and were rewarded with a piece of land to settle on at the end of the term

Multiple Choice

10. Whose military reforms were instrumental in the rise of powerful generals?

    a. Cornelius Sulla   b. Gaius Marius
    c. Pompeius Magnus   d. Crassus

11. Who did not want their land taken away and redistributed to small landowners?

    a. soldier-farmers   b. the plebians
    c. the Gracchi brothers   d. the Senate

Constructed Response

12. What kind of social reforms did Tiberius and Gaius Gracchus try to make and why? Why did their attempts fail? Use details from the reading selection to support your answer.

    _____

    _____

    _____

    _____

    _____

The Republic of Rome Part 4: Julius Caesar

In 46 B.C., Gaius Julius Caesar became sole dictator of Rome for life. However, he was killed by a group of conspirators in 44 B.C.

Conquest of Gaul

Julius Caesar (100–44 B.C.) can be considered one of the best military commanders of all time. His most significant accomplishment was the conquest of Gaul. The **annexation** of Gaul changed the whole concept and character of the Roman state. Roman civilization now incorporated not only the lands around the Mediterranean but also western Europe. (See map on page 39.)

Gaul was made up of a number of Celtic tribes. In 58 B.C. during the First Triumvirate, Caesar became governor of the provinces of Cisalpine Gaul (northern Italy), Illyricum (east of the Adriatic Sea), and Narbonese Gaul (southern France). He decided to march northward and make the whole area into a Roman province, because he claimed that the tribes posed a threat to the Gallic provinces. Some maintain, however, that his attack on the Gauls was due to his own ambition and desire to increase his military prestige. So started the **Gallic War** (58–51 B.C.). The account of the war was reported by Julius Caesar himself in his book *De Bello Gallico.*

Cleopatra

After the Gallic War, Caesar became involved in the civil war against Pompey, whom he defeated in Greece in 48 B.C. In 47 B.C. Caesar went to Egypt where he met **Cleopatra**, and they became lovers. After Caesar helped her defeat the king of Egypt, he made Cleopatra queen of the land. Egypt also became a client state of Rome. Then Caesar returned to Italy, where he was made dictator of Rome for life in 46 B.C.

Caesar's Reforms

During his **dictatorship**, Caesar accomplished much and devoted his career to reforms. One of his most important reforms was the establishment of colonies in Italy and the provinces to deal with the ongoing problem of the urban poor and the landless ex-soldiers. The **colonies** were small settlements for war veterans intended as a reward for their loyalty. Civilians, specifically the unemployed poor of the cities, were also allowed to live there. The colonies became important places of defense and acted as instruments in the **Romanization** of the provinces. Caesar also tackled the long-standing problem of debt. He erected a number of public buildings in Rome. He also revised the Roman calendar, which, with minor changes, is still used today.

Conspiracy Against Caesar

Due to the nature of his reforms, Caesar incurred the hostility of the upper class and the Senate. A **conspiracy** against him was planned and instigated by two leading members of the Senate, Cassius and Marcus Brutus. Eventually there were sixty conspirators. The murder happened when the Senate gathered for a meeting in Pompey's theater. There the conspirators cruelly stabbed Caesar to death. Caesar died on the **Ides of March** (March 15), 44 B.C.

Name: _____ Date: _____

Knowledge Check

Matching

_____ 1. annexation

_____ 2. Cleopatra

_____ 3. colonies

_____ 4. conspiracy

_____ 5. dictatorship

_____ 6. Gallic War

_____ 7. Ides of March

_____ 8. Romanization

a. Caesar made her Queen of Egypt

b. War against the Gauls to make the whole area a Roman province

c. government in which absolute power is concentrated in one person

d. bringing another country or territory within the power of a state

e. March 15; the middle of March

f. making the provinces more like Rome

g. plotting secretly against someone, often to take away their power or kill them

h. small settlements for war veterans intended as a reward for their loyalty

Multiple Choice

9. Which Roman leader did Caesar fight during the civil war?

    a. Pompey   b. Crassus

    c. Marcus Brutus   d. Cassius

10. Which of these provinces was Caesar NOT the governor of?

    a. Cisalpine Gaul   b. Egypt

    c. Illyricum   d. Narbonese Gaul

Constructed Response

11. What were Julius Caesar's accomplishments as dictator? Which of these do you think was most significant? Use details from the reading selection to support your answer.

_____

_____

_____

_____

_____

_____

_____

Octavian-Augustus: The First Roman Emperor

The Second Triumvirate

After Caesar's death, his right-hand man, **Mark Antony**, tried to gain control of the situation. At the same time, **Octavian**, who was the grand-nephew and adopted heir of Caesar, also rose to power with the support of the Senate. In 43 B.C. both generals and one of Caesar's military commanders, **Lepidus**, established the second Republican coalition of three dictators to rule the Roman state. This was called the **Second Triumvirate**.

Both Antony and Octavian proceeded to fight Caesar's murderers, Brutus and Cassius, and defeated them in 42 B.C. in two battles at Philippi in Macedonia. It was then decided by both leaders that Antony would control the eastern provinces and Octavian would control the western provinces.

Civil War Between Antony and Octavian

Soon tension between the two men started to grow because Antony had abandoned his wife, who was Octavian's sister, and was having an affair with Queen Cleopatra of Egypt. Jealousy and ambition were also factors in forcing the two dictators apart. About the same time, the third dictator, Lepidus, contested Octavian's supremacy in the West and, as a result, was forced to retire and was disarmed. As the years went by, the rivalry between Antony and Octavian increased until the third and final civil war of the Republic broke out. In 31 B.C. Octavian defeated Antony and his ally, Cleopatra, at the **Battle of Actium** on the west coast of Greece. Both Antony and Cleopatra fled to Egypt where they committed

Octavian defeated Mark Antony and Cleopatra's forces at the Battle of Actium and became the sole ruler of the Republic.

suicide. Octavian, in turn, conquered Egypt in 30 B.C. and made it a Roman province. (See map on page 39.)

Octavian Becomes Augustus

After the Battle of Actium, Octavian became the sole ruler of the Republic. He planned to restore Rome to its old glory and establish peace and stability after a century of war. In order to accomplish his goal, however, he had to form a new type of government that resembled the old Republic constitution but did not include its weaknesses. Learning from his predecessors' mistakes, he did not make himself a dictator. Instead, for his first years in power, he concealed his power behind republican traditions. In 27 B.C. he pronounced "the transfer of the state to the free disposal of the Senate and the people." This action earned him the reputation of being the restorer of the Republic, whereupon the Senate bestowed on him the title of **AUGUSTUS** (which means "the revered one") to define his new status as leader of the Roman state. He was known as Augustus thereafter. Augustus became the first **emperor** of the **Roman Empire**, which lasted from 27 B.C. to A.D. 476.

Thus, the outcome of the Battle of Actium was three-fold: (1) It was the end of the Roman Republic; (2) Octavian-Augustus became the master of the Graeco-Roman world; and (3) The Roman state was dominated by the West with Rome as the capital, while the East was kept in second place.

Augustus as Supreme Ruler

Even though Augustus retained many of the republican offices, such as the consulship and the Senate, he was the supreme ruler of the state. He embodied the roles of the president of the Senate, leader of the Roman army, and chief priest. He was granted power over the senatorial governors in the provinces and power as the tribune of the people. The courts, legislation, finance, and internal and foreign policy were all in his hands.

Augustus took extensive journeys and reorganized the Roman provinces. He made Egypt into a Roman province. He added the whole **Iberian Peninsula** (Spain and Portugal) to the empire, and he made Gaul into three new provinces. In the east he annexed Galatia in Asia Minor and made Judaea into a Roman province. Augustus' stepson, Tiberius, campaigned north of Italy and managed to extend the Roman territories to the Danube and Rhine Rivers, making the rivers the natural furthermost boundaries of the Roman Empire. (See map on page 39.)

In 27 B.C., Octavian was given the title Augustus and became the first emperor of the Roman Empire.

Augustus accomplished other deeds as well. He created a permanent bodyguard and a city police, which were stationed in Rome. He instituted a fire brigade. He founded a new military treasury from which he could pay his soldiers. He also embellished Rome with a number of public buildings, both restoring old ones and erecting new ones. This greatly pleased the people of Rome.

The Roman Peace

Augustus showed himself to be a great general and administrator in the reorganization of the government and the provinces. He transformed the shattered Republic into a new regime that was to last for many centuries. He solved the problem of governing by making the Roman state a one-man rule, accomplished in the appearance of the old republican traditions. He created a durable Roman peace, called the ***Pax Romana***, that lasted for two centuries, until A.D. 180. During this period there was no major war and the economy prospered. An extensive network of roads extending throughout the empire increased the flow of trade. Trade flourished in exports such as wool, olive oil, wine, metal work, and pottery. In return, Italy received goods from the provinces, including slaves, grain, marble, and ivory. Production from agricultural goods, rather than trade, however, provided the major part of Rome's total revenue.

A year before Augustus died, he made a will that included a summary of the military and financial resources of the empire and a political testament of his achievements. This testament is called the "Res Gestae Divi Augusti" or "Acts of Achievement of the Divine Augustus" and provides historians with an important document of Augustus' life and accomplishments.

The Julio-Claudian Dynasty

To ensure that the rule of the empire stayed in the hands of men of his choice, Augustus arranged his own **successors** to the throne by adopting them as his sons. As the years went by, he chose several candidates, but they either died in battle or were poisoned to death. When Augustus died, the only remaining candidate, his stepson Tiberius, succeeded him as the next emperor.

Augustus ruled Rome for 44 years and died in A.D. 14. For the next half century, the empire was ruled by four members of Augustus' family, known as the **Julio-Claudian Dynasty**. Augustus's successor was Tiberius (14–37). Then Caligula (37–41), Claudius (41–54), and finally, Nero (54–68) succeeded to the throne.

Name: _____ Date: _____

Knowledge Check

Matching

_____ 1. Augustus

_____ 2. emperor

_____ 3. Lepidus

_____ 4. Mark Antony

_____ 5. Julio-Claudian Dynasty

_____ 6. Iberian Peninsula

_____ 7. Pax Romana

_____ 8. successors

_____ 9. Roman Empire

a. peace that lasted for two centuries

b. Spain and Portugal

c. Augustus and members of his family who ruled the Roman Empire from 27 B.C. to A.D. 68

d. title that means "the revered one," given to Octavian

e. those who follow as a ruler or in an office

f. the leader of an empire

g. one of Caesar's military commanders who was part of the Second Triumvirate

h. territories and people under the rule of the Romans

i. member of the Second Triumvirate who had been Caesar's right-hand man

Multiple Choice

10. Who did Octavian defeat at the Battle of Actium?

    a. Antony and Lepidus

    c. Cassius and Lepidus

    b. Brutus and Cassius

    d. Antony and Cleopatra

11. Who was NOT a member of the Julio-Claudian Dynasty?

    a. Nero

    c. Tiberius

    b. Pompey

    d. Claudius

Constructed Response

12. How did Octavian, unlike his predecessors, manage to become sole ruler and first emperor of the Roman world? Use details from the reading selection to support your answer.

_____

_____

_____

_____

_____

_____

_____

Notable Emperors:
The Early Roman Empire A.D. 14–180

Nero

Claudius

The last two emperors of the Julio-Claudian Dynasty were notable for their actions. Claudius (A.D. 41–54) was known for his activities in the provinces. He was responsible for incorporating Britain as a province into the Roman Empire. Mauritania, in Africa, and Thrace, north of Greece, were also added as Roman provinces during his reign. (See map on page 39.) Claudius adopted his stepson, Nero, to succeed him on the throne.

Nero

Nero (54–68) is considered one of the worst emperors to rule Rome. Upon his **accession** to the throne, he quickly lost interest in public affairs. He preferred to be involved in pleasure activities such as music, drama, races, and sexual activities. His rule is also known as the "reign of terror," because he suspected many members of the Senate of conspiracy and put them to death. Nero even killed some members of his own family, including his mother. In A.D. 64 a great fire swept through Rome. Nero blamed the small Christian community for the fire. As a result, many of the Christians were persecuted and killed. It was thought, however, that Nero himself had planned the fire. In fact, right after the fire had destroyed much of the city, he started building a new imperial palace that was decorated with gold. It was called the "Golden House" and extended over a large part of the city. Nero's unpopularity increased in the last years of his reign when he started appearing in public performances. He went on an artistic tour of Greece where he participated in many of the games, winning all the first-place prizes. Finally, the army, neglected by the emperor, killed him.

Following Nero's murder, revolts led by different Roman armies broke out in the provinces. This led to a short period of civil war (68–69) in which four emperors ruled the state. The last of the four emperors, Vespasian, brought stability back to the empire.

The Flavian Dynasty

Vespasian, succeeded by his two sons, Titus and Domitian, belonged to the **Flavian Dynasty** of rulers (69–96). Vespasian and Titus ruled the empire well. A Jewish revolt in Judaea was suppressed in A.D. 70 with the capture and destruction of Jerusalem. Both emperors concentrated on the reconstruction of the empire and strengthening its defenses. In Rome, a lot of money was spent on public works—most notably the **Colosseum**, which was a large arena where gladiatorial fights were held. One noted event during the short reign of Titus was the eruption of the volcano **Vesuvius**, near Naples in A.D. 79. Ash from the volcano buried two nearby towns, Pompeii and Herculaneum, and wiped out most of the population. Vespasian's other son, Domitian, was not a popular ruler. He was a second Nero. He ruled the empire with a stiff hand, neglecting the Senate. This caused dissatisfaction among the Senate's members. Afraid for his life, Domitian put many of the Senate's leading members to death. His unpopularity cost him his life at the hands of a member of his bodyguard and his own wife.

The Golden Age

The next century was dominated by the "**Five Good Emperors**." This period of the second century A.D. was considered the "**Golden Age**" of the Roman Empire. Most notable of the five emperors were Trajan (98–117), Hadrian (117–138), and Marcus Aurelius (161–180).

Trajan

Trajan came from Spain and was the first emperor to come from a province. This symbolized the start of provincial men rising to power within the ruling classes of Rome. Trajan was popular with both the Senate and the people. Even though he had absolute control of the state, he put on a good show toward the Senate with his diplomacy. He is best remembered for his military conquests and public works in Rome and the provinces. Trajan conquered a region called Dacia, north of the Danube River, and annexed it to the empire. He also fought the Parthians in the east and annexed Armenia, Mesopotamia, and part of Arabia to the Roman Empire. No emperor had gone this far and none would go beyond. The Roman Empire, in terms of territorial expansion, reached its largest extent during Trajan's reign. (See map on page 51.) Trajan's many public works, paid for by the booty from Dacia, adorned Rome and the provinces. One of these was the Column of Trajan in Rome, around which the story of Trajan's achievements in Dacia was carved in a spiral decoration. Trajan's good rule in Rome and abroad earned him the title of "**Optimus Princeps**" or "Best Ruler."

Trajan's Column in Rome

Hadrian

Hadrian succeeded Trajan as emperor. Hadrian dealt extensively with troubles within the provinces. In fact, he spent more than half his reign outside of Rome, traveling throughout the provinces. Because the provinces of the east, newly acquired by Trajan, were difficult to hold and defend, Hadrian abandoned them and withdrew back to the Euphrates River as the eastern bound-

ary of the Roman Empire. Hadrian also strengthened the Roman boundaries in the west by building defensive walls along the Rhine and Danube Rivers as well as a wall in Britain, which was named after him. **Hadrian's Wall** marked the northernmost extent of Roman occupation in Britain and the empire as a whole. Hadrian's main goal was to stabilize the Roman Empire. He is also known for the construction of public buildings in the provinces as well as a private palace surrounded by gardens and pools in Tivoli, just outside Rome.

Hadrian's Wall in Great Britain

Marcus Aurelius

Marcus Aurelius was the last of the "Five Good Emperors," and his death brought an end to the Pax Romana created by Augustus. He was known as the "philosopher-king," because he was deeply involved with philosophical thoughts that he wrote down in a book called *Meditations*. During most of his reign, Marcus Aurelius was involved in the defense of the Roman Empire, fighting against the Parthians in the east and the German tribes who started to break through the frontier along the Danube River. (See map on page 51.) In addition, a plague struck the empire, killing many civilians and soldiers. The loss of life caused by wars and natural disasters resulted in a man shortage. This led to large numbers of Germans being admitted into the empire as settlers and **auxiliary** soldiers along the boundaries. These Germans helped the Romans in the defense of the empire against other German tribes who started to threaten the frontiers on a larger scale. In addition to the man shortage, the wars were costly and resulted in financial problems. Defending the borders of the empire, not the conquest of additional territory, now became the primary concern for the emperor and his Roman army. This meant more money was being spent than was coming into the empire. Thus, ecomonic as well as political stability began to decline in the Roman Empire.

Knowledge Check

Matching

_____ 1. accession
_____ 2. auxiliary
_____ 3. Colosseum
_____ 4. Flavian Dynasty
_____ 5. Golden Age
_____ 6. Hadrian's Wall
_____ 7. Optimus Princeps
_____ 8. Vesuvius

a. built in Britain, it marked the northenmost extent of the Roman Empire

b. volcano that buried Pompeii and Herculaneum

c. the act of coming into a high office

d. Vespasian and his two sons

e. title meaning "Best Ruler"

f. used as a reserve or backup

g. period of the Roman Empire in the second century A.D.

h. large arena where gladiatorial fights were held

Multiple Choice

9. What was the new imperial palace that Nero built called?

a. Golden House
c. Colosseum

b. Senate
d. Column of Trajan

10. Which of these men was NOT one of the Five Good Emperors?

a. Hadrian
c. Marcus Aurelius

b. Trajan
d. Domitian

Constructed Response

11. Why was the second century A.D. regarded as the "Golden Age" of the Roman Empire? Use details from the reading selection to support your answer.

_____

_____

_____

_____

_____

_____

Name: _____ Date: _____

Map Follow-Up

Directions: Using an atlas and the map below, find and list all the modern-day countries that would have been included in the Roman Empire at its greatest extent in A.D. 120.

_____

_____

_____

_____

_____

_____

_____

_____

Expansion of the Roman World 218 B.C.–A.D. 120

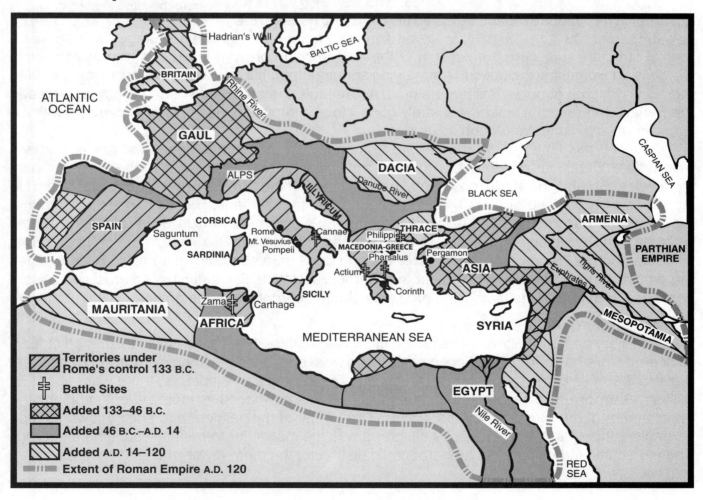

Notable Emperors:
The Late Roman Empire
A.D. 180–305

After a period of civil war following the death of Commodus, Septimius Severus became emperor.

Commodus

Marcus Aurelius was succeeded by his son, Commodus (180–192). Commodus was another emperor like Nero. He is regarded as one of the most eccentric of Rome's emperors because he was addicted to emotional religions and gladiatorial sports. His relations with the Senate were hostile, and this led him to execute many of its members. Finally, the head guard of the imperial bodyguard commissioned a professional athlete to murder him.

Septimius Severus

As happened after Nero's death, a civil war followed for four years (193–197). In 193 a rich senator and two provincial governors were all hailed as the emperor of Rome at the same time. Eventually, Septimius Severus from North Africa, who was the provincial governor in the Danube region, defeated his rivals and became the sole emperor (193–211). Septimius Severus made a number of significant changes in the governmental structure to secure the position of the emperor and prevent disorder and rebellion within the state. In Rome, he excluded the remaining senators from his administrative positions and filled them with knights of purely military training. As a result, the so-called sharing of power between the Senate and emperor was now entirely gone. He also replaced the imperial bodyguard with his own Danubian soldiers and doubled its size.

During this time the **defense** of the Roman Empire became a bigger and graver problem than before. Septimius Severus added more provincial natives as soldiers to the army, increasing its size. He also initiated steps to make the officers of the army a **privileged** social class. He increased their pay and rewards by increasing the taxes on civilians. These changes indicate that the army had become the sole basis of the emperor's power. Septimius Severus died in Britain while on a military campaign in 211. On his deathbed, he advised his sons to "be on good terms with one another, be generous to the soldiers and don't care about anything else." Septimius left the empire jointly to his two sons, Geta and Caracalla. Until 235, Septimius Severus' successors continued to deal with the increasing problems along the frontiers of the empire.

Barrack Emperors

Military anarchy followed for a period of 50 years (235–284). This is called the period of "**barrack emperors**." A series of soldier emperors who were appointed and then overthrown by different provincial armies came to the throne. Along with the 27 "regular" emperors, there were about 50 military **usurpers** who assumed the imperial title. Rome now faced its most serious problem: the appointment of the emperors by the armies. The loyalty of the soldiers had shifted towards their generals rather than the state. Above all, greed was the motive for frequently changing emperors. The more gifts and rewards an emperor could distribute, the more loyalty the soldiers showed.

During this 50-year period, the situation along the frontiers deteriorated. Invasions of Germanic tribes along the northern border and the new Persian Sassanid Empire along the eastern border posed an increasing threat to the empire. As a result, the Romans abandoned Dacia, and the boundary was brought back to the Danube River. (See maps on pages 51 and 61.) Both the internal wars and frontier battles had a lasting effect on Rome's stability.

By 284, within fifteen years, the military situation had recovered and the empire was temporarily restored. However, the economy within the empire had collapsed. The imperial treasury was depleted, old taxes were increased, new taxes were raised, and inflation was at an all-time high. Moreover, trade declined, and Rome became entirely dependent on imported goods from the east, hardly exporting any goods of its own. Many farms were abandoned, and on the farms where production of goods continued, there was no increase in productivity because there was no technological improvement. Rome's social situation also collapsed due to a decline in population. The middle class disappeared and lower-class farmers suffered tremendously.

Diocletian

The emperor who came to power after this 50-year period of civil war was Diocletian (284–305). He was temporarily able to restore a measure of stability to the empire. Diocletian was the greatest imperial organizer since Augustus. He tried to deal with the deteriorating military and economic situation of the Roman Empire by introducing a number of reforms.

In order to deal with the military situation, which was impossible for one emperor to handle, as well as to insure an orderly series of imperial successions, Diocletian partitioned the empire into a government ruled by four people. This was known as the ***tetrarchy***. He appointed a second ruler as co-emperor of the state and two Caesars as secondary emperors who would succeed the emperors upon their deaths. Diocletian and his Caesar, Galerius, ruled the eastern half of the empire, and Maximian and his Caesar, Constantius, ruled the western half. Diocletian also reorganized the empire by increasing the number of provinces from 50 to 100, making them smaller in size with each un-

Diocletian divided the rule of the Roman Empire among four people. This was known as the tetrarchy.

der a provincial governor. The provinces were grouped into thirteen major units, called ***dioceses***, each ruled by governors. In turn, the dioceses were grouped under four ***prefectures***, each under an administrator called a prefect. (See map on page 61.) In doing so, he made the governing of the empire more efficient and insured little opportunity for internal revolts. Diocletian also restructured the Roman army by creating two branches: a mobile field force and a frontier force.

In an attempt to restore the economic situation, Diocletian issued an edict of prices that fixed the maximum prices on all goods and transportation costs, as well as the maximum wages for all workers throughout the empire. He made an attempt to stabilize the coinage and made the process of tax collecting more systematic. However, he was not able to lessen the burden of taxation on the Roman people because he needed the money to carry out his reforms.

To sum up, Diocletian created a **totalitarian** state in order to maintain the imperial defenses and stop economic decline. The Senate had disappeared. In 305 Diocletian stepped down from his throne due to health reasons, and he forced Maximian to do the same. Galerius and Constantius became co-emperors in their place.

Name: _____ Date: _____

Knowledge Check

Matching

_____ 1. barrack emperors

_____ 2. defense

_____ 3. dioceses

_____ 4. prefectures

_____ 5. privileged

_____ 6. tetrarchy

_____ 7. totalitarian

_____ 8. usurpers

a. when the Roman Empire was ruled by two co-emperors and two Caesars

b. a series of soldier emperors appointed and overthrown by different provincial armies

c. the 13 major units the provinces were grouped in

d. the four units that were each administered by a prefect

e. keeping danger or attack away

f. those who tried to take the title without a legal right

g. government where one leader or small group has strict control over everything

h. those with special benefits or not subject to the usual rules

Multiple Choice

9. Who was NOT a member of the tetrarchy?

   a. Constantius

   b. Septimius Severus

   b. Diocletian

   d. Maximian

10. Who did Septimius Severus appoint to administrative positions?

   a. senators

   b. slaves

   c. military knights

   d. gladiators

Constructed Response

11. What type of change did Septimius Severus make in the structure of the Roman government? Why did he make this change, and what effect did it have on the position of the emperor? Use details from the reading selection to support your answer.

_____

_____

_____

_____

_____

_____

_____

The Rise and Spread of Christianity

Christianity

Christianity originated in the eastern Roman Empire in the first century A.D. It began as a sect of Judaism in Palestine, in the Roman province of Judaea, with the birth and death of Jesus. The life and teachings of Jesus would alter the course of western history. For two centuries, Christianity spread slowly throughout the Roman Empire. The early spread of Christianity can be largely attributed to Paul, a Jew from the Greek city of Tarsus in Asia Minor. During the first half of the first century, Paul traveled throughout the eastern part of the empire spreading the gospel of Jesus.

Later, through other people's missionary work, Christianity spread throughout the rest of the Roman world. It was first adopted among the urban-dwellers in the big cities of the empire, including Rome. During the third century, Christian communities throughout

Paul of Tarsus helped spread Christianity to the Roman Empire.

the empire grew at a rapid rate due to the insecurities of the time. The people of the Roman Empire had lost faith in the state and were seeking individual and personal salvation. To satisfy this religious quest, the people turned to the sacramental religion of Christianity. Christianity was also popular because it offered the emotional satisfaction of religious love and preached the equality of all people. It was a literate religion that accepted Classical culture and, as a result, also attracted the educated members of the empire.

The Roman State Religion

The official religion of the Roman Empire was the Roman state religion, which, like the Greeks', involved the worship of many gods. It was a **polytheistic** religion and is known as **paganism**. The Romans also worshipped the emperor as a god. The Roman state tolerated any religion that did not threaten the tranquility and safety of the empire. As long as the people participated in the worship of the emperor and the state religion, the Roman state did not interfere in their private lives. The Christians, however, refused to worship the Roman gods and the emperor. As a result, during the first three centuries A.D., the Christians were regarded as traitors and were persecuted by the Roman emperors.

Persecution

Persecutions of Christians had started under Nero, when they were blamed for the big fire of Rome that occurred in A.D. 64. They continued to be carried out on a small scale by Domitian, Marcus Aurelius, and Septimius Severus. The persecution culminated in the reigns of Diocletian and Galerius, between 303 and 311. This was known as the "Great Persecution of Christians." Then, in 311 Galerius issued the **Edict of Sophia**, an edict of tolerance in favor of Christianity. Christianity was legalized in the eastern half of the Roman Empire.

Constantine the Great

After the resignation of Diocletian and Maximian, the planned succession of the tetrarchy broke down in confusion. By 310, there were five emperors ruling the Roman Empire. Among the rulers was Constantine the Great (306–337) who eventually emerged as the sole ruler of the empire.

Constantine had succeeded Constantius in 306 as ruler of the western half of the empire. Constantine defeated, one by one, the other rival emperors. In 312 he defeated Maxentius in the **Battle of the Milvian Bridge** in Rome and became sole ruler of the western half of the empire. At this battle, Constantine asserted that his victory over Maxentius was due to a miracle. According to his biographer, Eusebius, just before the battle Constantine saw a flaring cross in the sky and the following inscription: BY THIS SIGN THOU SHALT CONQUER. The sign was the Christian XP (Chi-Rho) sign, which he put on the shields of his soldiers. In this way, Constantine became the first Christian emperor of the Roman Empire, although he was not baptized until the moment of his death. In 324 Constantine defeated his remaining rival in the East, Licinius, and became the sole ruler of the Roman Empire. (See map on page 61.)

Constantine legalized Christianity throughout the Roman Empire and was baptized a Christian on his deathbed.

Legalizing Christianity

During his reign, Constantine the Great initiated a series of measures favoring the Christians. In 313 he issued the **Edict of Milan**, which legalized Christianity throughout the empire. He exempted Christian clergy from any secular obligations, such as paying taxes. Imperial funds were used to subsidize the building of churches in the provinces. In addition, Constantine took steps to defend Christianity by taking actions against current heresies that had emerged. In the fourth century, separate movements within Christianity developed due to disputes and controversies in the doctrines of the Christian belief; most notable of these was **Arianism**. Arianism was founded by Arius, an Egyptian priest from Alexandria who disputed the positions of the three individuals of the Trinity (God the Father, the Son, and the Holy Spirit). Arius and his followers believed that the three individuals of the Trinity were not equal, unlike the Christian belief. In 325 Constantine tried to resolve the dispute by calling a meeting of church leaders at the Council of Nicaea. This meeting produced the **Nicene Creed**, which declared Arianism a **heresy**. In short, Constantine was responsible for the conversion of the empire from paganism to Christianity.

Constantinople

In regard to the domestic affairs of the empire, Constantine continued to carry out the reforms begun by Diocletian. He tightened control of the empire and increased taxation. He continued to reorganize the army by increasing the proportion of German troops and elevating them to high positions. When Rome was no longer capable of serving as the capital of the Roman Empire due to its distant location from the boundaries, Constantine founded a new capital. He built the new capital on the Greek town of Byzantium, located on the Bosporus Strait, and renamed it **Constantinople** (present-day Istanbul). Constantinople was ideally located to supervise both the northern-Danube and eastern-Euphrates defenses.

Christianity continued to flourish under Constantine's successors. In the reign of Theodosius I (378–395), Christianity took another important step forward. Theodosius became known as "the Great" because he insisted on the rigorous practice of Christian orthodoxy. He suppressed any remnant of paganism and Arianism, and by the end of his reign (394), Christianity was made the official religion of the Roman Empire.

Christianity was one of the most important Roman legacies to Western civilization.

Name: _____   Date: _____

Knowledge Check

Matching

_____ 1. Christianity

_____ 2. paganism

_____ 3. polytheistic

_____ 4. Arianism

_____ 5. Edict of Sophia

_____ 6. Battle of the Milvian Bridge

_____ 7. Edict of Milan

_____ 8. heresy

_____ 9. Constantinople

a. an edict that legalized Christianity

b. religion that originated in Judaea with the life of Jesus; focused on personal salvation

c. where Constantine defeated Maxentius after placing the XP sign on his soldiers' shields

d. religion where many gods are worshipped

e. the new capital of the Roman Empire founded by Constantine

f. a belief that the three individuals of the Trinity were not equal

g. an edict of tolerance in favor of Christianity

h. having many gods

i. an opinion contrary to what the church teaches

Multiple Choice

10. The state religion required the Romans to worship who as a god?

a. the best gladiator

b. the emperor

c. the apostle Paul

d. the mayor of Rome

11. Even though Constantine was considered the first Christian emperor, what did he not do until the moment of his death?

a. read the Gospels

b. adopt the XP sign

c. get baptized

d. legalize Christianity

Constructed Response

12. Why did Christianity spread so rapidly throughout the Roman Empire and eventually become the official Roman state religion? Use details from the reading selection to support your answer.

_____

_____

_____

_____

_____

_____

The Fall of the Roman Empire
A.D. 337–476

Vandals Plundering Rome

The Western and Eastern Empires

After the reign of Constantine, the Roman Empire declined rapidly. After the reign of Theodosius in 395, the empire was permanently split into two parts, the western half and the eastern half, each with a different emperor who acted independently from the other. (See map on page 61.) When historians talk of the fall of the Roman Empire, they only mean the western half of the empire. The Western Roman Empire held on for less than a century until its collapse in the fifth century. The Eastern Roman Empire survived for a thousand years longer and was known thereafter as the **Byzantine Empire**.

Germanic Invasions

The immediate cause for the fall of the Western Roman Empire was the Germanic invasions across the Roman frontiers. The Romans had continuously battled Germanic tribes for some time. However, during the fourth and fifth centuries, the Germans started to cross the borders and invade the empire on a massive scale. (See map on page 62.)

The Germans were a loosely knit group of people, organized into a number of different tribes that the Romans had to fight individually. Along the Rhine River, the Franks, the Vandals, and the Burgundians threatened the empire's borders. Along the Danube River, the Goths posed a dangerous threat to the empire. The Goths were divided into two states, the **Ostrogoths** (eastern Goths) and the **Visigoths** (western Goths).

The massive Germanic invasions were triggered by the movement of another tribe of barbarians, called the **Huns**, who probably lived in northern China. By 370 the Huns had moved west into the Balkan area and entered the Danube River basin, conquering the Ostrogoths along the way. As a result, the Visigoths were terrified and were driven across the Danube River into the Roman Empire where they settled in 376.

The Visigoths

Because of their unjust treatment at the hands of the Romans, the Visigoths revolted and ravaged northern Greece. In 378, the Roman emperor, Valens, dealt with the crisis and met them in a battle at Adrianople in Thrace. For the first time, the Roman army was defeated by a Germanic tribe, and Valens was killed. This battle is regarded as one of the worst defeats the Roman army ever experienced. The Battle of Adrianople was a decisive battle because it marks the beginning of Germanic invasions into the Roman Empire on a massive scale. It also showed the Germans that the Roman army was not invincible.

After the battle, the Visigoths were pacified and were allowed to settle within the borders of the Roman Empire living under their own leaders. Under their leader, Alaric, the Visigoths moved west and invaded Italy several times and finally sacked Rome in 410. The Visigoths eventually moved to Spain where they set up their own kingdom in 418.

Germanic Tribes Set Up Their Own Kingdoms

While dealing with the Visigoths in 406, the Roman army had to abandon both the Rhine River and British frontiers. This left the borders open, and the Vandals, the Burgundians, and the

Franks invaded the empire, plundering many Roman towns along the way. At first, the Romans made a treaty with the different Germanic tribes and granted them **federal status** within the empire. This meant that they were allowed to live under their own rulers, but had to supply the Romans with soldiers and farmers. They became allied to the Romans. Eventually, the different tribes openly ruled their own states and tore themselves away from Roman control. The Vandals moved into Spain and then Africa, where they set up their own kingdom in 439. The Burgundians settled along the Rhone River in southern Gaul in the 430s. The Franks inhabited northern Gaul and unified into the Frankish kingdom in 481.

The Huns

In the meantime, the Romans also had to deal with the Huns, who had become another threat to the empire. By the early fifth century, the Huns had built up an empire from the Baltic Sea to the Danube River. In 434 **Attila** became their leader. He ruled for 19 years and was known as the "Scourge of God" because he played a large part in the downfall of the Western Roman Empire. In 451 Attila marched into Gaul where he met a combined army of Romans and federate Germans in a battle at Chalons on the Marne River. Attila was defeated, and he had to evacuate Gaul. However, in the following year Attila decided to cross the Alps into Italy and attack Rome. His plan failed, and Attila withdrew from Italy. In 453, he died, and his empire fell apart.

Attila the Hun was known as the "Scourge of God."

The End of the Western Roman Empire

By the middle of the fifth century, the Western Roman Empire was coming to an end. For the last twenty years, the empire was ruled by many emperors who had become mere puppets on the throne. Their election depended solely on powerful German generals in the army. Finally, in 476 the last emperor of the Roman West, **Romulus Augustulus**, was overthrown by a German general called **Odovacar**. Odovacar was proclaimed King of Italy by his soldiers. Italy became the last Germanic kingdom. Several Germanic kingdoms in the west and the Byzantine Empire in the east replaced what once was the mighty Roman Empire.

The Roman army, superior in numbers and equipment, had dealt with the Germans for a long time, defeating them in many battles over the years. Why then were the barbarian invasions in the fifth century successful in destroying the Western Roman Empire? The underlying causes had their roots in the late Roman Empire. Politically, there was internal disunity. One of the prime causes of disunity was the failure of emperors to control the army and its generals, which led to numerous civil wars. The emperors were not able to secure peaceful succession to the throne. As a result, the emperors could not successfully defend the imperial borders. In addition, because of the man shortage in the army, more and more Germans were recruited as soldiers and generals. These German recruits proved to be less dependable and loyal to the Roman state than Roman soldiers. Economically, the Roman Empire was drained. During the last three centuries of rule, the prime concern of the emperors was the defense of the Roman frontiers rather than expansion. This meant that more and more was spent on the army while less and less money was coming into the empire. Taxes continued to increase, which resulted in the rise of inflation. The stagnation of technology and decrease in trade were also major factors in the decline of Roman power. All these factors affected the empire socially. The people became poorer and dissatisfied, which destroyed individual loyalty toward the Roman state. The Germanic invasions of the fourth and fifth centuries merely sped up the process of collapse in the Western Roman Empire.

Name: _____ Date: _____

Knowledge Check

Matching

_____ 1. Byzantine Empire

_____ 2. Ostrogoths

_____ 3. Visigoths

_____ 4. Huns

_____ 5. federal status

_____ 6. Attila

_____ 7. Romulus Augustulus

_____ 8. Odovacar

a. a tribe of barbarians from Asia that moved into Europe

b. the last emperor of the Western Roman Empire

c. the western Goths

d. the eastern Goths

e. German general who overthrew Romulus Augustulus and was proclaimed King of Italy

f. leader of the Huns; called the "Scourge of God"

g. another name for the Eastern Roman Empire

h. Germanic tribes were allowed to live under their own rulers, but they had to supply the Romans with soldiers and farmers.

Multiple Choice

9. Why did the Visigoths cross the Danube River and settle within the Roman Empire?

    a. they wanted to get away from the Huns

    b. the Ostrogoths forced them out of the Balkan area

    c. they had run out of food

    d. they were invited by the Romans

10. Who was killed at the Battle of Adrianople?

    a. Romulus Augustulus

    b. Odovacar

    c. Valens

    d. Attila

Constructed Response

11. Why were the Romans not able to defeat the Germans in the fifth century despite their superiority in numbers and equipment? Use details from the reading selections to support your answer.

_____

_____

_____

_____

_____

_____

_____

Name: _____   Date: _____

Map Follow-Up

Directions: Use the map below to list the dioceses located in the Eastern Roman Empire and the Western Roman Empire.

Eastern Roman Empire: _____

_____

_____

Western Roman Empire: _____

_____

_____

The Roman Empire A.D. 400

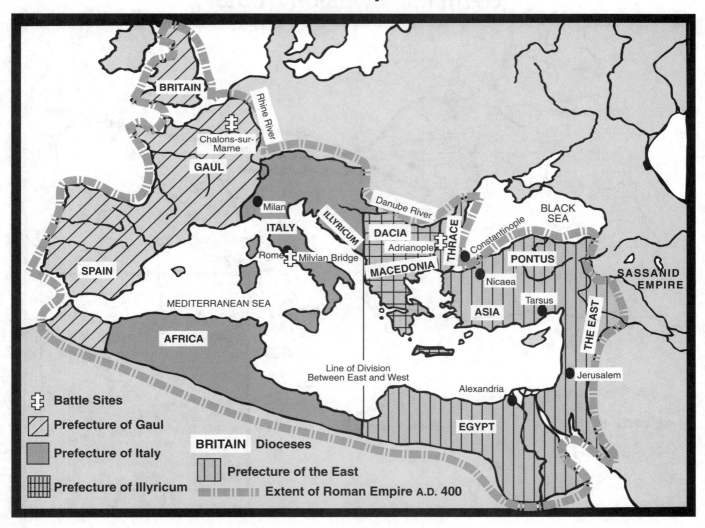

Name: _____   Date: _____

Map Follow-Up

Directions: Use the map below to answer the following question.

What was the situation in the Mediterranean region after the collapse of the Western Roman Empire in the fifth century?

_____

_____

_____

_____

_____

_____

Germanic Invasion Routes

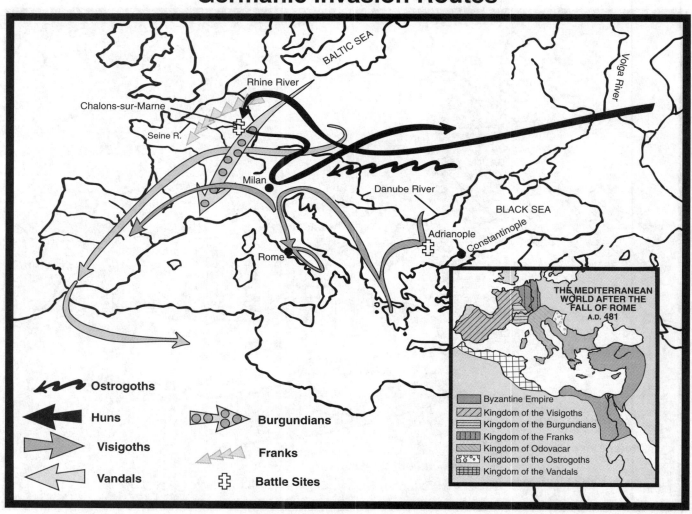

Roman Architecture

Structures in the City of Rome

The surviving architecture in Rome today is testimony to its grandeur in the days when it was the capital of the Roman Empire. Rome, located on the Tiber River and surrounded by seven hills that provide a naturally protected site, controlled the whole Mediterranean world for many centuries.

The buildings that embellished Rome at the peak of its power during the Imperial period were numerous and impressive. These included theaters, baths, temples, libraries, imperial palaces, basilicas or public

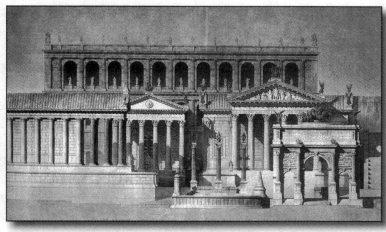

The forum was the chief marketplace of Rome. It also contained temples, basilicas, the Senate House, and public monuments to the emperors.

meeting places, fora (plural of forum) or commercial and social centers of the city, and arenas for public events. Public monuments commemorating the achievements of emperors, such as triumphal arches and columns, were also erected. Bridges, aqueducts (artificial channeling systems for conducting water to the city), and a strong defensive wall with access gates completed the array of public structures that once adorned the city of Rome. These types of monuments and structures could be found in any Roman city throughout the empire.

The Forum

The nucleus of a Roman city was the *forum,* an area of open space that served as the commercial and social center where people met to socialize and businesses sold their goods. Law courts were also located there. A forum consisted of a central, open, rectangular space surrounded by basilicas, which were long, open structures supported by columns, and a temple. The greatest and oldest forum in the Roman world was the Forum Romanum, the chief marketplace of Rome. It was unusual in that it was not built in one phase, but grew in size through the years. It was filled with basilicas, temples, the Senate House, and the triumphal arch of Septimius Severus.

Concrete

During the Late Republic period, the Romans invented a new building material that we still use today. By mixing volcanic dust and lime mortar, they produced a cement that hardened into **concrete**. The Romans used it as the core for the walls of buildings. Because concrete was unattractive to the eye, they faced it with marble slabs or baked clay bricks. The many surviving Roman monuments throughout western Europe testify to the strength and durability of concrete.

The Romans adopted several architectural features from the Etruscans and the Greeks. They adopted the form of the arch from the Etruscans. From the Greeks, they used the classical orders of the Greek temple, most commonly the Corinthian architectural order. The Romans developed and combined these elements with the use of concrete to form their own unique architectural style.

The Etruscan Arch

The Romans made great use of the Etruscan **arch**. The Etruscans used it as a single stone structure to build gateways in their fortification walls. But the Romans used the arch in various ways, and in combination with the use of concrete, created architectural structures of great size and strength. They created the *vault* by putting a series of arches side by side. A *dome* was created by several arches crossing in different directions in a circular space that intersected in the center. The use of arches and concrete revolutionized Roman architecture. New ways of exploiting the interior space of buildings were developed, thus creating monuments of great size and complexity.

There are many examples of these arch structures in Rome and the provinces. The most simple use of the arch can be seen in the construction of city gates, bridges, and aqueducts. Bridges consisted of a series of arches joined in a line and were built across valleys and rivers. Many are still in use today. An **aqueduct** consisted of one to three levels of joining arches through which water was channeled into a city. Vaulted arches were used in the construction of triumphal arches commemorating the achievements of the Roman emperors. The walls were carved with sculpted reliefs of the emperors' triumphs, sacrifices, and battles. Corinthian columns also decorated the outside of the archways.

Arches and Greek columns were also used in the construction of theaters and **ampitheaters** (round theaters). The most famous example of such a monument was the Colosseum in Rome. Arches were used throughout the building to support the different levels of the seating area. The outer facade consisted of three stories of arches, decorated with Greek columns in between each of the arches. Arches, vaults, and domes were used in the construction of the imperial palaces and public buildings, such as baths, to create vast interior spaces.

Greek Columns

The Greek influence in Roman architecture can be seen in the form of columns on the outer facades of the aforementioned monuments, but it can most easily be noticed in the construction of basilicas and temples with the use of Corinthian-style columns. A **basilica** was a long portico supported by a series of columns. It served as an open-air, public meeting place. A typical **Roman temple** consisted of a closed structure built on a high platform. The temple structure, in most cases, had a deep, columned porch in the front. Sometimes it was surrounded entirely by columns, as in a Greek temple.

One of the most impressive and fully preserved examples of the Roman ability to exploit interior space in conjunction with the use of Greek columns was the Pantheon. The **Pantheon**, built by Hadrian, was a temple dedicated to all gods. The building was made of solid concrete and consisted of a round main room topped by a dome. It was fronted by a porch of Corinthian columns. The interior of the temple was lavishly painted and decorated with gold.

Private Homes

The private dwellings of the Romans were of two types. The common people lived in tightly packed apartment buildings, much like today. The wealthier Romans built large townhouses, furnished with numerous rooms and a garden. The center of the typical Roman house was the *atrium* or living room, which was surrounded by the other rooms of the house. These included the kitchen, bedrooms, dining room, and store rooms. At the end of the house was a small garden. Because the houses had very few and small windows, the sloping roof of the houses had a hole right above the center of the atrium, called the *compluvium,* where light and air could enter. The rain water would be collected below in a pool, called the *impluvium,* which was the same size as the hole. It was common for two rooms in the front of the house on either side of the main entrance and fronting the street to be used as shops. The Romans decorated their houses with elaborate frescoes and mosaics depicting scenes of everyday life.

Examples of the Architecture
of the Roman Empire

Roman Bridge

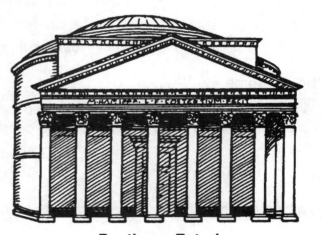

Roman Aqueduct

Roman Triumphal Arch

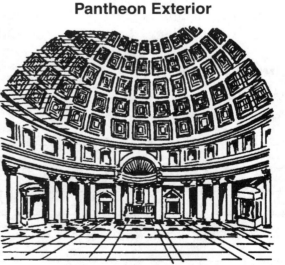

Pantheon Exterior

Roman Townhouse

Pantheon Interior

Name: _____ Date: _____

Knowledge Check

Matching

_____ 1. forum

_____ 2. concrete

_____ 3. arch

_____ 4. aqueduct

_____ 5. ampitheater

_____ 6. basilica

_____ 7. Roman temple

_____ 8. Pantheon

a. one to three levels of joining arches through which water was channeled into a city

b. a temple built by Hadrian and dedicated to all gods

c. used by the Etruscans as a single stone structure for gateways in their walls

d. a mixture of volcanic dust and lime mortar that hardened into a strong, durable building material

e. an area of open space that served as the commercial and social center of a Roman city

f. a long portico supported by a series of columns

g. a round theater

h. a closed structure built on a high platform, usually with a deep columned porch in the front

Multiple Choice

9. What architectural structure was formed by several arches crossing in different directions in a circular space that intersected in the center?

    a. vault

    c. impluvium

    b. aqueduct

    d. dome

10. Which architectural structure was not part of a Roman townhouse?

    a. impluvium

    c. compluvium

    b. basilica

    d. atrium

Constructed Response

11. What Roman invention revolutionized Roman architecture? Use details from the reading selection to support your answer.

_____

_____

_____

_____

_____

_____

Name: _____ Date: _____

Explore: Make a Mosaic

Romans decorated their homes, courtyards, public buildings, and works of art with mosaics. **Mosaics** are pictures or designs made by setting small colored pieces of stone, tile, or glass into soft cement. Mosaics might be simple geometric designs or more elaborate pictures of fish, birds, animals, gods, or heroes. Mosaics are still used today. Use the steps below to design and make your own mosaic.

Materials Needed: Large sheet of heavy cardboard, sheet of paper, pencil, scissors, modeling clay, modeling knife, tempera or acrylic paints, bowl, paintbrush, rolling pin, ruler, plaster of Paris, spreader, sponge

Step One: On a sheet of paper, create your design. A simple geometric design is the easiest.

Step Two: Copy your design or picture onto the sheet of heavy cardboard.

Step Three: Roll out the clay until it is about $\frac{1}{8}$-inch thick. Using the ruler, cut the clay into squares. The size of the squares will depend on the size of your design. A square between $\frac{1}{4}$-inch and $\frac{1}{2}$-inch is ideal. Larger designs require larger squares, and smaller designs require smaller squares. Smaller squares enable you to make more elaborate and intricate designs.

Step Four: After the tiles have dried, paint them different colors.

Step Five: When the paint has dried, decide which color you are going to use for each part of your design by placing the tiles directly on the design on the cardboard. You will need to move the tiles around to see what arrangement looks best. You may even decide to make some changes in your design to accommodate the tiles.

Step Six: Prepare the plaster of Paris according to the package directions. Carefully spread the plaster on the cardboard, a little bit at a time. Press your tiles into place while the plaster of Paris is still wet. Since the plaster will cover your design as you apply it, it is important that you put it on in small amounts. As you look at the part of the design that is not covered and the original drawing you did on your sheet of paper, you will be able to see where the tiles should be placed.

Step Seven: After the mosaic is dry, use a sponge or dry cloth to wipe away any residue from the plaster of Paris.

Alternative Method of Making a Mosaic

If you would prefer a simpler method that takes less time and materials, use squares of construction paper and glue to make the mosaic. The same basic ideas apply.

Roman Entertainment

The Colosseum

Many grisly events were held for the entertainment of the Roman people in the Colosseum. Built in the reigns of Vespasian and his sons, the **Colosseum** was a building of tiered arches that supported seating areas for 45,000–55,000 people. Below the center stage of the structure were underground rooms and cages where wild beasts and the participants of the events were kept before the games began. There was also a water system that allowed for the flooding of the stadium in order to carry out mock sea battles.

Model of the Circus Maximus and the Colosseum

Gladiators

One of the main events held in the Colosseum was the hand-to-hand combat between **gladiators**, trained fighters who might be slaves or free men. Gladiatorial fights were first performed as part of a religious ritual at Etruscan funerals. The Romans began using these contests as entertainment for the people. It was a way for Roman emperors to control the people by satisfying their lust for action and bloodshed. At the start of the fights, the gladiators shouted together to the emperor: "We who are about to die salute you." Then the fights began. Gladiators usually fought each other until one of them was killed. Sometimes, however, a gladiator would only wound his opponent. If a victim fell wounded, he could ask for mercy from the emperor. The emperor would listen to the pleas of the crowd and decide the fate of the victim with a signal of his thumb. If the emperor gave the **thumbs-up sign**, the victim lived. If he pointed the thumb downward, the victim would be killed.

Executions

Another form of entertainment was the execution of criminals by wild beasts. Unarmed, helpless human beings were thrown to wild lions and bears. When the Christians were persecuted during the reigns of Nero, Domitian, and Diocletian, they were also thrown to the wild beasts.

Chariot Races

Chariot races were held at the **Circus Maximus**, a 700-yard-long oval stadium that could hold about 150,000 people. The chariots were drawn by two, three, or four horses. Even though these races were not as gruesome as the gladiatorial fights, crashes were common, and some charioteers were trampled to death by approaching horses and chariots.

Roman Baths

Romans also relaxed at the Roman baths, called *thermae*. These were not just places to cleanse oneself, but were also places for social gatherings. Wealthy Romans often spent whole days at the baths. The Romans did not use soap to wash themselves, like today. Instead their bodies were rubbed with oil. The oil with the dirt was then scraped off with a *strigil*, which was a blunt razor-like tool. Men and women alike spent the day being bathed by slaves, exercising, discussing news, and playing games with their friends. A Roman bath house was a large structure with a changing room, a swimming pool, and four different kinds of baths: a cold room, a warm room, a hot room, and a dry sweating room. The baths were heated by steam from an underfloor heating system, called a *hypocaust*. By the Imperial period, the more elaborate bath houses included libraries, art galleries, shops, gymnasiums or exercise areas, and gardens.

Name: _____ Date: _____

Knowledge Check

Matching

_____ 1. Colosseum

_____ 2. gladiators

_____ 3. thumbs-up sign

_____ 4. chariot races

_____ 5. Circus Maximus

_____ 6. thermae

_____ 7. strigil

_____ 8. hypocaust

a. signal from the emperor to let the victim live

b. an underfloor heating system for the baths

c. a 700-yard-long oval stadium for chariot races

d. a round building of tiered arches with seating for 45,000–55,000 people

e. races where people drove small carts pulled by two, three, or four horses

f. trained fighters who might be slaves or free men

g. a blunt razor-like tool for scraping off oil and dirt

h. name for the Roman baths

Multiple Choice

9. Who were killed by wild beasts for the entertainment of the people?

   a. soldiers

   c. slaves and servants

   b. criminals and Christians

   d. Senators

10. Which was NOT a type of bath at a Roman bath house?

   a. a dirt bath

   c. a dry sweat

   b. a cold bath

   d. a hot bath

Constructed Response

11. Why did the emperors think it was important to provide entertainment for the people? Use details from the reading selection to support your answer.

_____

_____

_____

_____

_____

_____

_____

_____

The Roman Army

The Romans were able to conquer most of the ancient world and control vast territories and peoples for nearly a thousand years by means of its basic fighting force, the army. The army was the force behind the growth and greatness of Rome.

A Roman soldier was armed with a short sword, a dagger, and a javelin. He was protected by armor, a helmet, and a shield.

An Army of Citizens

During most of the Republic period, before the first century B.C., the Roman army was recruited from the citizen body in times of war. The citizens were grouped into units of one hundred men each, called *centuries*. The army was organized according to social and economic classes. The wealth of each man determined in which century he fought. The wealthiest citizens served in the cavalry, because they could afford the full armor, whereas the poorest citizen, not being able to afford much protection, made up the light-armed troops.

The Professional Army

In the first century B.C., the consul Marius reorganized the Roman army by making it a professional army. All citizens, especially the poor and unemployed, were able to join the army for a wage and become professional soldiers, serving the Roman state for 16 years. Marius' military reforms made the army more flexible and interchangeable, eliminating the earlier army division according to economic and social classes.

The professional Roman army was an organized body of soldiers and officers that was divided into several units. The largest unit of the Roman infantry was the *legion*, which numbered between 4,000 and 6,000 men. The legion was divided into ten *cohorts*. Each cohort was divided into six *centuries.* Sixty centuries made up a legion. The Roman legions varied in number between 28 and 33 during the Imperial period.

Command of the Army

The commander in chief of all legions was the *imperator,* who was also the emperor during the Imperial period. Each legion was commanded by a *legatus,* or commanding general, who was helped by six *tribuni.* The backbone of the legion was the *centurion,* who commanded the centuries (60 in number). Other officers included the second-in-command of the centurion, the standard-bearer, and the *tessarius,* who was responsible for the watchword.

The legions were drawn up for battle in a three-line formation. The first line consisted of young soldiers (*hastati*), the second line consisted of experienced soldiers (*principes*), and the third line was made up of veteran soldiers (*triarii*). Each was armed with a sword and spear for close-range combat. Every legion also had its own corps of specialists and its own cavalry. The cavalry was an auxiliary unit of the Roman army. The corps of specialists included writers, accountants, engineers, carpenters, and surveyors. These men were used to build roads and bridges, select the camps, and do the accounts.

Auxiliary Units

The *auxilia,* or auxiliary army units, consisted of the light-armed troops and the cavalry. Men in the auxilia were recruited primarily from the provinces. The auxilia were divided into cohorts of 500 or 1,000 men each, which in turn were divided into centuries. These forces supported the legions in battle. The auxiliary infantry unit was used to fight in front of the legions and used similar weapons as the legionary soldier. It also included soldiers with special functions such as archers or slingers. On the flanks of the legions fought the cavalry cohorts, consisting of about 120 men on horseback, called *alae* or wings. The auxiliary forces also served on the frontiers patrolling and defending the empire's borders.

Life in the Army

During the Imperial period, a Roman soldier served in the army for 20 years. Life in the army was hard and busy. The soldiers were either fighting or training. The pay was little, and each soldier had to pay for his own food and clothing. The meals were rudimentary and consisted of porridge, bread, cheese, beans, and wine.

Uniform and Weapons

The uniform of the legionary soldier was a linen vest over a woolen tunic. Over these garments was metal body armor. He wore a brown cloak that could be used as a blanket during cold periods. Sandals with hobnails were worn on the feet. A helmet and a large shield protected him on the battle field. The weapons used for fighting were a short sword, a dagger, and a javelin. At the end of his service, each soldier received a retirement payment and a plot of land, usually in colonies along the frontiers, where he was still called upon for duty to defend the empire in times of trouble.

The Romans were invincible for a long time, not only because of their trained and organized army, but also because of the siege weapons that they used in siege warfare. Mobile towers, ramps, and scaling ladders were used to besiege a city. The most impressive machine of all was the catapult, called the *ballista,* which hurled rocks and flaming darts against the enemy.

Army Camps

The Roman army set up temporary camps during campaigns. Camp was set up in a square area that was surrounded by a ditch. Behind this a mound and a rampart were built. On top of the rampart stood a palisade. Two main streets ran north-south and east-west through the camp. The commanding general's quarters was at the center of the camp, known as the *praetorium.* Other quarters included the soldier's barracks, the paymaster's quarters where prisoners, hostages, and booty were kept, and a forum that was the center of camp life.

Along the frontiers in the provinces, permanent camps, called *castra,* were set up. They were similar in plan to the temporary camps but permanent buildings were used. In addition to the soldiers' barracks, the general's quarters, and paymaster's quarters, the castrum included a hospital, storerooms, and baths.

Defending the Borders

During the late Imperial period when defending the frontiers rather than expanding the empire became the sole concern of the emperors, home recruitment began to decline. Emperors increasingly enrolled provincials and Germans, who had settled within Rome's borders, in the legions. By the time of Diocletian's reign, the previously unparalleled efficiency of the Roman legion was gone. In order to deal with the threatening situation along the borders, Diocletian and later Constantine changed the structure of the Roman army. The army was divided into two major branches: a mobile field force, consisting mostly of a cavalry, and a frontier force, which was permanently stationed along the border fortifications.

By the fifth century A.D., the Roman army was no longer able to stop the barbarian hordes from invading, and the Roman Empire collapsed.

Name: _____ Date: _____

Knowledge Check

Matching

_____ 1. legion
_____ 2. cohorts
_____ 3. centuries
_____ 4. auxilia
_____ 5. alae
_____ 6. ballista
_____ 7. castra
_____ 8. praetorium
_____ 9. tessarius

a. groups of about 120 men on horseback who fought on the flanks or sides of the legions

b. permanent camps set up along the frontiers in the provinces

c. ten of these made up a legion; it was divided into six centuries

d. an officer responsible for the watchword

e. units of 100 men; the backbone of the legion

f. the largest unit of the Roman army; 10 cohorts or 60 centuries

g. the commanding general's quarters at the center of the camp

h. auxiliary army units; the light-armed troops and the calvary

i. a catapult that hurled rocks and flaming darts

Multiple Choice

10. Of the following commanders, who was the commander in chief of all the legions?

    a. tribuni
    c. imperator
    b. centurion
    d. legatus

11. What were the veteran soldiers in a legion's third line called?

    a. alae
    c. hastati
    b. principes
    d. triarii

Constructed Response

12. Why was the Roman army able to conquer and control such a large area and its people for nearly a thousand years? Use details from the reading selection to support your answer.

_____

_____

_____

_____

_____

_____

_____

_____

Name: _____ Date: _____

Explore: Identify Parts of a Soldier's Uniform

Directions: On the diagram below, label the following items that a Roman soldier would have as part of his uniform and weaponry.

dagger   **armor**   **shield**   **javelin**
helmet   **sandals**   **short sword**

1. _____

2. _____

3. _____

4. _____

5. _____

6. _____

7. _____

Name: _____ Date: _____

Greek and Roman Map Activity

Directions: Locate the following places or areas on the map below by placing the number of the item on the corresponding line on the map. Use the maps from this book, an atlas, or the Internet if you need help.

Greek Civilization

1.	Athens	2.	Sparta	3.	Knossos	4.	Mycenae
5.	Macedonia	6.	Ionia	7.	Troy	8.	Crete
9.	Euphrates River	10.	Alexandria	11.	Marathon (battle)		
12.	Thermopylae (battle)			13.	Babylon		

Roman Civilization

14.	Rome	15.	Rhine River	16.	Danube River	17.	Sicily
18.	Cannae (battle)	19.	Actium (battle)	20.	Carthage	21.	Constantinople
22.	Gaul	23.	Zama (battle)	24.	Adrianople (battle)	25.	Britain

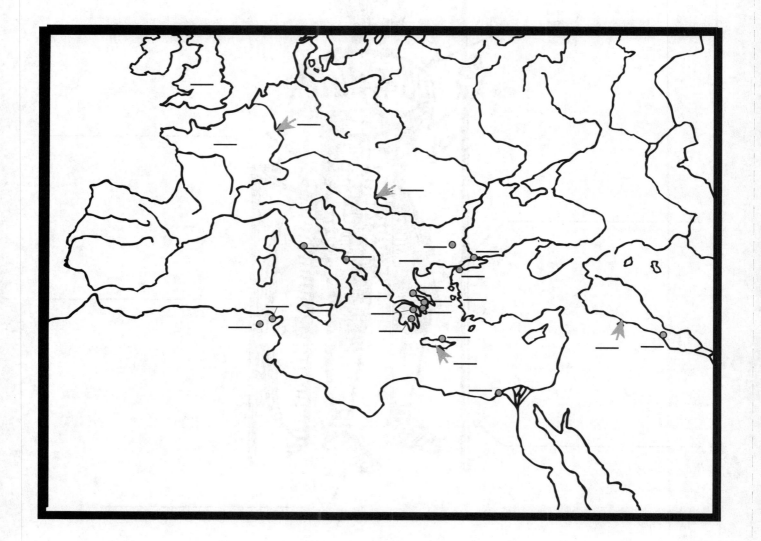

Glossary

accession – the act of coming into a high office

Acropolis – the sacred hill in Athens dedicated to Athena

aedile – office of public relations in Rome that organized festivals and other events

Agora – the commercial and political center of Athens

alae – groups of about 120 men on horseback who fought on the flanks or sides of the Roman legions

Alexander the Great – son of Philip II of Macedon who conquered the Persian empire; considered one of the greatest conquerors in world history

Alexandria – finest of the cities named for Alexander the Great, located on the Nile Delta in Egypt

Alps – high, snow-covered mountains in northern Italy

ampitheater – a round theater

annexation – bringing another country or territory within the power of a state

aqueduct – one to three levels of joining arches through which water was channeled into a city

arch – used by the Etruscans as a single stone structure for gateways in their walls; the Romans used arches in various ways to create larger, more complicated structures

architecture – the art or science of designing and building structures

archons – two leaders of the government in Athens who held the executive power

Areopagus – the hill in Athens where the council of elders met

Arianism – a belief that the three individuals of the Trinity were not equal; founded by the Egyptian priest Arius

Asia Minor – modern-day Turkey

assembly – a council of Spartan people who could reject or approve proposals put before them

atrium – the living room or center of a typical Roman townhouse

Attila – leader of the Huns; called the "Scourge of God"

Augustus – title, meaning "the revered one," bestowed on Octavian by the Roman Senate to define his new status as leader of the Roman state

auxilia – auxiliary army units in the Roman army that consisted of the light-armed troops and the cavalry

auxiliary – used as a reserve or backup

ballista – a catapult that hurled rocks and flaming darts

barrack emperors – a series of soldier emperors appointed and overthrown by different provincial armies in the Roman Empire (A.D. 235–284)

basilica – a long portico supported by a series of columns; served as an open-air, public meeting place

Battle of Actium – (31 B.C.) Sea battle where Octavian defeated Mark Antony and his ally Cleopatra

Battle of Cannae – (216 B.C.) battle where Hannibal destroyed a whole Roman army

Battle of the Milvian Bridge – (A.D. 312) where Constantine defeated Maxentius after placing the XP sign on his soldiers' shields

Black Figure pottery – the figures were drawn in black on a red background

bronze – a metal alloy of copper and tin; used to make tools, weapons, and body armor

bull-leaping – Minoan sport where people jumped onto a bull by grabbing its horns, did a somersault over the bull, and landed back on the ground

Byzantine Empire – another name for the Eastern Roman Empire centered on Constantinople

Carthage – a colony of the Phoenicians located on the coast of North Africa; fought three wars with Rome called the Punic Wars

castra – permanent camps of the Roman army set up along the frontiers in the provinces

centuries – units of 100 men; the backbone of the Roman legion

centurion – the commander of a Roman century

chariot races – races where people drove small carts pulled by two, three, or four horses

chorus – group of performers in Greek drama who danced and sang at intervals throughout the play

Christianity – religion that originated in Judaea with the life of Jesus; focused on personal salvation

Circus Maximus – a 700-yard-long oval stadium for chariot races

city-state – a small independent political unit in Greece based around a city; polis

Cleopatra – Caesar made her Queen of Egypt; she was Caesar's lover and later Mark Antony's lover

clientes – poorer people, ex-slaves, and newcomers to Rome

cohorts – ten of these made up a Roman legion; it was divided into six centuries

coinage – a system of money

colonies – small settlements for Roman war veterans intended as a reward for their loyalty; usually located in the Roman provinces

Colosseum – large arena in Rome where gladiatorial fights were held

comedies – plays that made fun of political or social issues at hand

compluvium – an open hole in the roof of a Roman townhouse where light and air could enter

concrete – a mixture of volcanic dust and lime mortar that hardened into a strong, durable building material

conspiracy – plotting secretly against someone, often to take away their power or kill them

Constantinople – the new capital of the Roman Empire founded by Constantine; it had been called Byzantium and is today Istanbul

consuls – two men who held the executive power in the Roman Republic

Corinthian order – style of column that featured a capital with acanthus leaves

Cornelius Scipio – Roman general who defeated Hannibal

Cornelius Sulla –a powerful Roman general who put down a rebellion in Asia Minor and then marched on Rome, starting the First Civil War

council of elders – 28 ex-magistrates in Sparta who gave advice to the current magistrates

Crassus – Roman general who put down a slave rebellion led by Spartacus; became a member of the First Triumvirate with Pompey and Caesar

Dark Ages – period in Greek history from about 1200 to 750 B.C. when knowledge of art, architecture, and writing disappeared, trade declined, and the Mycenaean palaces were abandoned

defense – keeping danger or attack away

Delian League – organization of city-states led by Athens; set up to protect Ionia and Greece from the Persians

democracy – rule by the people; first developed in Athens

demos – Greek word for the people

dictatorship – government in which absolute power is concentrated in one person

dioceses – the 13 major units the Roman provinces were grouped in

dome – structure created by several arches crossing in different directions in a circular space that intersect in the center

Doric order –style of column that featured a plain capital

drama – telling a story through actors and dialogue

dromos – long tunnel-like entrance to a Mycenaean burial chamber

Edict of Milan – (A.D. 313) edict issued by the Roman emperor Constantine that legalized Christianity

Edict of Sophia – (A.D. 311) an edict issued by the Roman emperor Galerius in favor of Christianity

emperor – the leader of an empire

ephors – Greek word for a Spartan judge who dealt with internal and foreign affairs

Erectheion – temple on the Acropolis dedicated to both Athena and Erechteus (a legendary king of Athens)

Etruscans – group that settled in the area north of Rome between the Tiber and Arno Rivers known as Etruria and had a confederation of 12 city-states

federal status – Germanic tribes were allowed to live under their own rulers, but they had to supply the Romans with soldiers and farmers

festival – event in Greece that consisted of a procession and sacrifices to the god being honored and that was also a social occasion

First Punic War – (264–241 B.C.) war between Carthage and Rome over a conflict of interest in Sicily

First Triumvirate – (60–53 B.C.) a coalition in which Pompey, Crassus, and Caesar shared power to govern the Roman Republic

Five Good Emperors – (A.D. 96–180) Nerva, Trajan, Hadrian, Antoninus Pius, and Marcus Aurelius

Flavian Dynasty – Vespasian and his two sons

fleet – a group of ships

forum – an area of open space that served as the commercial and social center of a Roman city

Forum – central marketplace of Rome

frescoes – wall paintings

Gaius Gracchus – attempted to pass the same reforms as his brother Tiberius in 123 B.C.; also killed by the Roman Senate

Gaius Julius Caesar – Roman general with victories in Spain and Gaul who became a member of the First Triumvirate with Pompey and Crassus; defeated Pompey and was appointed dictator of Rome for life

Gaius Marius – became consul of Rome in 107 B.C.; created a professional Roman army

Gallic War – (58–51 B.C.) war against the Gauls to make the whole area a Roman province

Gauls – barbarians in the area north of Italy and in western Europe

gladiators – trained fighters who might be slaves or free men; they performed for the entertainment of the Roman people

Golden Age – period of the Roman Empire in the second century A.D. when there was peace and prosperity; time of the Five Good Emperors

Greek colonization – period where Greek colonies were set up along the coasts of southern Italy, Sicily, France, Spain, and along the coast of the northern Aegean and Black Seas

Greeks – citizens of Greece; those who settled in the area south of Rome known as Magna Graecia

Hadrian's Wall – built in Britain during Hadrian's rule, it marked the northernmost extent of the Roman Empire

Hannibal – brilliant general who led the Carthaginians

hastati – young soldiers in the first line of a Roman legion's battle formation

Hellenic – having to do with the Greeks

Hellenistic civilization – culture influenced by the Greeks from 336–30 B.C.

Hellespont – narrow strait of water connecting the Sea of Marmara and the Aegean Sea

helots – conquered people who were slaves who worked the land to supply food for the Spartiates

Hephaisteion – a temple in the Agora dedicated to the god of crafts, Hephaestus

heresy – an opinion contrary to what the church teaches

hippodrome – a stadium designed for equestrian (horse) events

Homer – first known Greek poet, who lived about 700 B.C.

hoplite – a heavily armed Greek soldier

Huns – a tribe of barbarians from Asia that moved into Europe by about A.D. 370

hypocaust – an underfloor heating system for the Roman baths

Iberian Peninsula – Spain and Portugal

Ides of March – March 15; the middle of March; Caesar was killed on March 15, 44 B.C.

imperator – the commander in chief of all the Roman legions; the emperor during the Imperial period

impluvium – a pool below the opening in a Roman townhouse where rainwater was collected

Indus River – the eastern boundary of Alexander the Great's empire

Ionian Migrations – during the Dark Ages, Greeks moved across the Aegean Sea to the western coast of Asia Minor

Ionian Revolt – Greeks in Asia Minor rebelled against their Persian rulers in 499 B.C.

Ionic order – style of column that featured a capital with ram's horns and egg-and-dart pattern

Iron Age – period when iron was used for making tools and weapons

Julio-Claudian Dynasty – Augustus and members of his family who ruled the Roman Empire from 27 B.C. to A.D. 68

King Darius III – ruler of the Persian empire who was defeated by Alexander the Great

King Minos – legendary king who lived on the island of Crete in the palace at Knossos

King's Peace – when the King of Persia imposed a temporary peace among the Greek city-states

Knossos – large palace in north-central Crete belonging to the Minoan civilization

labyrinth – a maze

Latins – members of the Italic tribe who lived near Rome in the area called Latium

legatus – the commanding general of a Roman legion

legion – the largest unit of the Roman army; 10 cohorts or 60 centuries

Lepidus – one of Caesar's military commanders who was part of the Second Triumvirate

Lex Hortensia – Roman law passed in 287 B.C. that recognized a People's Assembly

Linear B – written language of the Mycenaeans; its characters consisted of lines and it was written on clay tablets

Lycurgus – semi-legendary leader of Sparta who established a number of social and political institutions in about 700 B.C.

magistrate – judge

malaria – disease that includes fever and chills and is spread by mosquitoes

Mark Antony – Caesar's right-hand man who was part of the Second Triumvirate; became Cleopatra's lover and was defeated by Octavian at the Battle of Actium in 31 B.C.

Minoan civilization – flourished on Crete between 2000 and 1450 B.C.; named after the legendary King Minos

Minotaur – a mythical beast with the head of a bull and the body of a human; lived in the labyrinth on Crete

Monarchy – period from 753 to 509 B.C. when Rome was ruled by kings

monarchy – rule by a king or queen

mosaics – pictures or designs made by setting small colored pieces of stone, tile, or glass into soft cement

Mycenaean civilization – warlike people with large palaces in the Peloponnese; by about 1500 B.C. had a prosperous civilization

necropoli – Etruscan cemeteries

Nicene Creed – produced by the church Council of Nicaea, it declared Ariansim a heresy

Octavian – the grand-nephew and adopted heir of Caesar who was part of the Second Triumvirate; defeated Mark Antony at the Battle of Actium and eventually became the first emperor of the Roman Empire

Odovacar – German general who overthrew Romulus Augustulus and was proclaimed King of Italy

oligarchy – rule by a few wealthy men

Olympeion – temple in Athens dedicated to the king of gods, Zeus

Olympic Games – athletic competition held every four years in honor of the Greek god Zeus

Optimus Princeps – Latin words meaning "best ruler"; title given to Trajan

oracle – priestess who would deliver advice from the gods in the form of a riddle

orchestra – the central area for acting in a Greek theater

ostracism – voting to banish any man deemed threatening

ostraka – Greek word for the potshards used to cast votes for ostracism

Ostrogoths – the eastern Goths, one group of German invaders

paganism – religion where many gods are worshipped

pankration – a mix of boxing, wrestling, and judo; one of the Olympic events

Pantheon – a Roman temple built by Hadrian and dedicated to all gods

Parthenon – temple dedicated to Athens' patron goddess Athena

patricians – the land-owning aristocracy in Rome

patroni – wealthy protectors in Roman society

Pax Romana – Latin words for the peace that lasted for two centuries in the Roman Empire

Peloponnese – the southern peninsula of Greece connected to the rest of the country by the Isthmus of Corinth

Peloponnesian League – organization of city-states led by Sparta

Peloponnesian War – war between Athens and Sparta that lasted 27 years

pentathlon – a five-part contest that included the discus throw, long jump, javelin throw, 200-meter run, and wrestling; one of the Olympic events

perioiki – people the Spartans had conquered who were freedmen but who were socially inferior to the Spartiates

phalanx – a tight formation of Greek soldiers

plague – an outbreak of contagious disease

playwright – a person who writes plays

plebeians – the common people of Rome; farmers and traders *polis* – Greek word for a city-state

polytheistic – having many gods

Pompey – Roman general with victories in Spain and Asia who became a member of the First Triumvirate with Caesar and Crassus

pontifex maximus – the Roman high priest

pottery – artform that uses clay to make pots, vases, etc., used to store and serve items and as art objects

praetor – Roman judge of the city

praetorium – the commanding general's quarters at the center of a Roman army camp

prefectures – the four units in the Roman Empire that were each administered by a prefect

principes – experienced soldiers in the second line of a Roman legion's battle formation

privileged – those with special benefits or not subject to the usual rules

professional Roman army – poor citizens were allowed to join the army for terms of 16 years and were rewarded with a piece of land to settle on at the end of the term

province – a country or region under the control of the Roman government

Pyrrhic War – war between the Romans and the Greeks in southern Italy and their allies from mainland Greece; named after the Greek King Pyrrhus

quaestor – Roman financial officer

Red Figure pottery – the figures were outlined in black and left red on a black-glazed background

redistributing – taking land from rich nobles and dividing it up among farmers

Remus – founder of Rome who was killed by his brother

Republic – the name given to the new Roman state governed by two consuls and the Senate

Roman Empire – territories and people under the rule of the Romans from 27 B.C. to A.D. 476

Roman temple – a closed structure built on a high platform, usually with a deep columned porch in front

Romanization – making the provinces more like Rome

Romulus – founder of Rome who killed his brother and became the first king of Rome

Romulus Augustulus – the last emperor of the Western Roman Empire

Royal Road – road that ran from Sousa to Sardis in the Persian Empire

Rule of Thirty – period when Sparta ruled Athens with a group of thirty tyrants

Samnites – the toughest Italic tribe the Romans had to face

sarcophagi – stone caskets

satrap – the governor of a Persian province

satrapies – provinces in the Persian empire

sculptor – one who carves or forms hard materials to produce three-dimensional works of art

Second Punic War – (218–201 B.C.) war between Carthage and Rome where Hannibal invaded Rome but was later defeated at the Battle of Zama

Second Triumvirate – Mark Antony, Octavian, and Lepidus form the second Republican coalition of three dictators to rule the Roman state

Senate – governing body of ex-magistrates who advised the consuls in the Roman Republic

skene – a building in a Greek theater where the actors could change and store their belongings

soldier-farmers – lost their property when they had to fight in the Roman army; became unemployed and poor

Spartacus – a professional gladiator who led a slave rebellion during the Roman Republic

Spartiates – Spartan people

strigil – a blunt razor-like tool for scraping off oil and dirt

subsistence – every man owned and cultivated his own small plot of land for individual survival

successors – those who follow as a ruler or in an office

temple – building that housed the statue of the patron-god or goddess and sometimes kept the offering made to that deity

tessarius – an officer responsible for the watchword in the Roman army

tetrarchy – when the Roman Empire was ruled by two co-emperors and two Caesars

theater – a semi-circular structure where plays were performed, usually built on the slope of a hill *thermae* – name for the Roman baths; included cold, warm, hot, and dry baths

Third Punic War – ended in 146 B.C. with Carthage being razed to the ground

thumbs-up sign – signal from the emperor to let the victim live

Tiberius Gracchus – a tribune of the people who proposed social reforms to the Roman Assembly of the People in 133 B.C., but he was killed by the Senate

totalitarian – government where one leader or small group has strict control over everything

tragedies – plays that dealt with myths and historical events

treasury – the money a nation has to carry out its operations

triarii – veteran soldiers in the third line of a Roman legion's battle formation

tribuni – one of six officers in the Roman army who helped each legatus

tribuni plebis – the tribune of the people who represented the people in government affairs in Rome

trireme – Greek ship powered by three sets of oars

Trojan Horse – hollow wooden horse that the Greeks hid inside and the Trojans were tricked into bringing inside their city gates

tufa – a volcanic rock that was soft and easy to cut

tumulus – a mound of earth covering a tomb

tyranny – rule by a man who had not taken power according to the constitution in a Greek city-state

tyrant – a ruler from the new Greek middle class who had not taken power according to the constitution

upper class – wealthy landowners

usurpers – those who tried to take the title of Roman emperor without a legal right

vault – structure created by putting a series of arches side by side

Vesuvius – volcano that buried the Roman cities of Pompeii and Herculaneum

Visigoths – the western Goths, one group of German invaders

Zama – battle where Scipio won a final victory over Hannibal

Answer Keys

Roman Numeral Activity (page ix)
1. 88
2. 2009
3. 702
4. 661
5. 930
6. 18
7. 44
8. 373
9. 456
10. 89

Knossos (page 2)
Matching
1. c   2. g   3. d   4. a   5. b   6. e   7. f
Multiple Choice
8. b   9. d
Constructed Response
10. The frescoes have scenes of animals, religious festivals, and games, such as boxing and bull-leaping. There are no scenes of war. There is no evidence that the Minoans made weapons or built walls around their cities.

Mycenae (page 4)
Matching
1. f   2. d   3. g   4. a   5. c   6. e   7. b
Multiple Choice
8. a   9. c
Constructed Response
10. The Mycenaean palaces were surounded by well-built walls for defense. The frescoes showed scenes of hunting and warfare. Bronze weapons and body armor and ivory helmets were found. Tunnels were built to outside wells in case of a siege.

The Rise of Hellenic Civilization (page 7)
Matching
1. f   2. d   3. c   4. b   5. a   6. i   7. h
8. g   9. e
Multiple Choice
10. b   11. d
Constructed Response
12. Because Greece is a mountainous region, small independent political units developed rather than a large political union. Greeks loved freedom and independence. Each city-state had its own laws, constitutions, leaders, army, and system of taxation.

Lycurgus and Sparta (page 9)
Matching
1. f   2. d   3. e   4. a   5. c   6. g   7. b
Multiple Choice
8. d   9. b
Constructed Response
10. Wealth was not desirable and they did not want to be exposed to foreign behaviors and ideas. Because they could not travel or trade, they rarely learned anything new or learned how to get along with others. There was little individual freedom. They had to rely on what they could make or grow themselves, so they may have been less technologically advanced.

Athens and Democracy (page 11)
Matching
1. g   2. f   3. b   4. d   5. e   6. a   7. c
Multiple Choice
8. d   9. b
Constructed Response
10. The two governments were very different. The Athenians set up a democracy, or rule by the people. The Spartans were ruled by an oligarchy of a few powerful men. The Athenians had more freedom and even poor citizens could be elected to office. Both governments did try to distribute the land evenly among the citizens.

The Wars With Persia (page 14)
Matching
1. h   2. a   3. d   4. g   5. e   6. b   7. f
8. c
Multiple Choice
9. c   10. a
Constructed Response
11. The Athenian battle tactics allowed them to fight more effectively at Marathon. Then they were able to return to Athens in time to defend the city from the Persians.

The Peloponnesian War and Its Aftermath (page 17)
Matching
1. d   2. c   3. b   4. a   5. h   6. f   7. e
8. g
Multiple Choice
9. d   10. b
Constructed Response
11. Athens suffered from plagues and lost a third of its population, including its great leader Pericles. Athens lost control of its sea empire and lost its entire fleet. Athens' allies revolted and the treasury was empty. An oligarchic revolution also brought internal problems in the government.

Map Follow-Up (page 18)
The cities were separated by mountains and seas. It was easier to govern the local area centered around a city than try to hold together the whole Greek nation. Athens was known for its democracy. All of its citizens could participate in the government. Athens was also a center of culture and architecture. Sparta had an oligarchy where a few wealthy aristocrats held the power. Spartans were known as well-trained soldiers.

Alexander the Great (page 20)
Matching
1. d   2. b   3. g   4. e   5. a   6. f   7. c
Multiple Choice
8. d   9. b
Critical Thinking
Answers will vary. Answers should include details that support the student's position.

Map Follow-Up (page 21)
In any order: Greece, Macedonia, Albania, Montenegro, Serbia, Bulgaria, Turkey, Armenia, Azerbaijan, Syria, Lebanon, Israel, Jordan, Egypt, Saudi Arabia, Iraq, Kuwait, Iran, Afghanistan, Turkmenistan, Uzbekistan, Tajikistan, Pakistan, India

Greek Art and Architecture (page 25)
Matching
1. e   2. d   3. i   4. f   5. g   6. h   7. c
8. b   9. a
Multiple Choice
10. d   11. b
Constructed Response
12. A temple was like a cathedral or church because it was a building where a god was worshipped. Offerings given to the god were also stored there. The appearance of a temple was also like a cathedral because it was meant to be an impressive structure to honor the god and inspire the people. The builders tried to achieve perfection.

Explore: Identifying the Parts of a Greek Temple (page 26)
1. colonnade or peristyle
2. pronaos
3. cella or naos
4. cornice
5. frieze
6. column
7. stylobate
8. stereobate
9. geison
10. pediment
11. metope
12. triglyph
13. architrave
14. capital
15. shaft
16. frieze
17. architrave
18. volute
19. capital
20. capital
21. base
22. Doric Order
23. Ionic Order
24. Corinthian Order

Greek Theater and Games (page 29)
Matching
1. c   2. f   3. a   4. d   5. b   6. j   7. i
8. g   9. e
Multiple Choice
10. b   11. a

Constructed Response
12. Possible answers include: The modern games are not done to honor the gods. They are held in different cities each time. There are many more events, including separate winter games. Medals are given for first, second, and third place. Modern athletes do not compete in the nude. Women are allowed to compete.

The Etruscans and the Beginnings of Rome (page 32)
Matching
1. d   2. f   3. a   4. h   5. e   6. c   7. b
8. g   9. i
Multiple Choice
10. d   11. a
Constructed Response
12. The Etruscans had an organized government consisting of a confederation of 12 city-states, each with its own king. For many years, the Romans continued to have kings. The Etruscans passed on to the Romans the alphabet they adopted from the Greeks. While the Etruscans occupied Rome, it grew into a flourishing city.

The Republic of Rome Part 1: 509–218 B.C. (page 35)
Matching
1. f   2. d   3. g   4. a   5. i   6. h   7. b
8. e   9. c
Multiple Choice
10. a   11. d
Constructed Response
12. The patricians controlled the government because they were the only ones who could hold the office of consul or be a member of the Senate. They made all the important decisions. The plebians could not participate in the government, and their land was slowly taken from them. They were in a state of debt and servitude. By holding strikes and refusing to perform their duties to the state, they were eventually given certain rights.

Map Follow-Up (page 36)
First, from 509–280 B.C., they had to defeat the neighboring mountain tribes (Volsci, Aequi, Sabini), the Gauls, the Etruscans, the other Latin tribes, and the Samnites. Corsica was also acquired in 283 B.C.

Second, the Romans fought the Pyrrhic War against Greece from 280–275 B.C. Rome gained control over all the Greek city-states in southern Italy.

Third, they fought the First Punic War with Carthage from 264–241 B.C. Rome acquired Sicily and Sardinia.

The Republic of Rome Part 2: Hannibal
218–133 B.C. (page 38)
Matching
1. d   2. e   3. f   4. b   5. g   6. a   7. c
Multiple Choice
8. c   9. b
Constructed Response
10. New and more capable generals such as Scipio were chosen by the Romans. They were able to defeat the Carthaginians in Spain and prevent any reinforcements from reaching Hannibal in Italy. Then the Romans attacked Carthage, and Hannibal had to leave Italy to battle the Romans in Africa.

Map Follow-Up (page 39)
Two provinces in Spain, Sicily and Sardinia, Corsica, Africa, Macedonia-Greece, and Asia

The Republic of Rome Part 3: Civil Wars
133–46 B.C. (page 42)
Matching
1. d   2. h   3. i   4. c   5. f   6. g   7. a
8. e   9. b
Multiple Choice
10. b   11. d
Constructed Response
12. The Gracchi brothers tried to set a limit on the amount of property an individual could hold. They wanted to redistribute land to the poor citizens of Rome. Members of the Senate were wealthy landowners, and they didn't want to lose their property. The Senate had Tiberius and Gaius Gracchus killed.

The Republic of Rome Part 4: Julius Caesar
(page 44)
Matching
1. d   2. a   3. h   4. g   5. c   6. b   7. e
8. f
Multiple Choice
9. a   10. b
Constructed Response
11. Julius Caesar established colonies in Italy and the provinces where the urban poor and landless ex-soldiers could settle. The colonies were also used as places of defense and helped Romanize the provinces. He worked on the problem of debt, erected public buildings, and revised the Roman calendar. Answers will vary as to the most significant achievement.

Octavian-Augustus: The First Roman Emperor
(page 47)
Matching
1. d   2. f   3. g   4. i   5. c   6. b   7. a
8. e   9. h
Multiple Choice
10. d   11. b
Constructed Response
12. Octavian did not make himself dictator. He concealed his power behind republican traditions. He seemed to give up power and restore the republic when he transferred the state to "the free disposal of the Senate and the people." The Senate gave him the title Augustus to define his new status as leader of the Roman state. He was then the emperor.

Notable Emperors: The Early Roman Empire
A.D. 14–180 (page 50)
Matching
1. c   2. f   3. h   4. d   5. g   6. a   7. e
8. b
Multiple Choice
9. a   10. d
Constructed Response
11. Trajan expanded the empire to its largest extent. He was able to pay for public works with booty from Dacia. Hadrian strengthened Roman boundaries in the west and north with defensive walls. He stabilized the empire. He also built public buildings in the provinces. Marcus Aurelius was a philosopher-king and worked to defend the borders.

Map Follow-Up (page 51)
In any order: United Kingdom (Great Britain, Wales, Scotland), Netherlands, Belgium, France, Monaco, Spain, Portugal, Luxembourg, Germany, Czech Republic, Slovakia, Austria, Switzerland, Liechtenstein, Italy, San Marino, Hungary, Slovenia, Croatia, Bosnia-Herzegovina, Romania, Yugoslavia, Albania, Macedonia, Bulgaria, Greece, Moldova, Turkey, Georgia, Armenia, Azerbaijan, Iran, Iraq, Kuwait, Syria, Jordan, Lebanon, Israel, Saudi Arabia, Egypt, Libya, Tunisia, Algeria, Morocco

Notable Emperors: The Late Roman Empire
A.D. 180–305 (page 54)
Matching
1. b   2. e   3. c   4. d   5. h   6. a   7. g
8. f
Multiple Choice
9. b   10. c

Notable Emperors: The Late Roman Empire
A.D. 180–305 cont. (page 54)
Constructed Response

11. Septimius Severus only appointed knights of military training to administrative positions and excluded the senators. This stopped the sharing of power between the Senate and the emperor. He did this to prevent disorder and rebellion within the state. From then on, the emperor had total control of the goverment. However, the emperor had to treat the military well because he needed their support to stay in power.

The Rise and Spread of Christianity (page 57)
Matching

1. b   2. d   3. h   4. f   5. g   6. c   7. a
8. i   9. e

Multiple Choice
10. b   11. c

Constructed Response
12. Due to the insecurities of the time, people had lost faith in the state. They were seeking individual and personal salvation, so they turned to Christianity. It also offered the emotional satisfaction of religious love and preached the equality of all people. This appealed to the lower classes. Educated people liked that it was a literate religion that accepted Classical culture.

The Fall of the Roman Empire A.D. 337–476 (page 60)
Matching

1. g   2. d   3. c   4. a   5. h   6. f   7. b
8. e

Multiple Choice
9. a   10. c

Constructed Response
11. The emperors had become puppets on the throne depending on powerful generals in the army. The emperor could not control the army and its generals, which led to civil wars. They could not secure a peaceful succession to the throne. They were unable to defend the borders. German soldiers on the border were less dependable and loyal than Roman soldiers. All the money was spent on the army, but there was no new money coming in. There was no new technology and trade declined. The people were dissatisfied and felt no loyalty to the Roman state.

Map Follow-Up (page 61)
Eastern Roman Empire: Dacia, Macedonia, Thrace, Asia, Pontus, The East
Western Roman Empire: Italy, Illyricum, Gaul, Britain, Spain, Africa

Map Follow-Up (page 62)
The Western Roman Empire ceased to exist. There were several different kingdoms of German tribes. The Eastern Roman Empire became known as the Byzantine Empire with its capital at Constantinople.

Roman Architecture (page 66)
Matching
1. e   2. d   3. c   4. a   5. g   6. f   7. h
8. b

Multiple Choice
9. d   10. b

Constructed Response
11. The Romans invented concrete, which was a durable and strong building material. They combined the use of concrete with architectural features, like the arch borrowed from the Etruscans and columns from the Greeks.

Roman Entertainment (page 69)
Matching
1. d   2. f   3. a   4. e   5. c   6. h   7. g
8. b

Multiple Choice
9. b   10. a

Constructed Response
11. The emperors thought they could control the people by providing entertainment that satisfied their lust for action and bloodshed. If they didn't satisfy the people, the emperors feared the people would turn against them.

The Roman Army (page 72)
Matching
1. f   2. c   3. e   4. h   5. a   6. i   7. b
8. g   9. d

Multiple Choice
10. c   11. d

Constructed Response
12. The army was made up of Roman citizens, so they felt loyalty to the generals and the state. When the army became a professional army, all citizens could join and get a wage. This eliminated the division between rich and poor and allowed the soldiers to work together better. The army was well organized, and for most of the imperial period, it was well supplied and cared for.

Explore: Identifying Parts of a Soldier's Uniform (page 73)
1. helmet   2. armor
3. dagger   4. short sword
5. shield   6. javelin
7. sandals

Greek and Roman Map Activity (page 74)

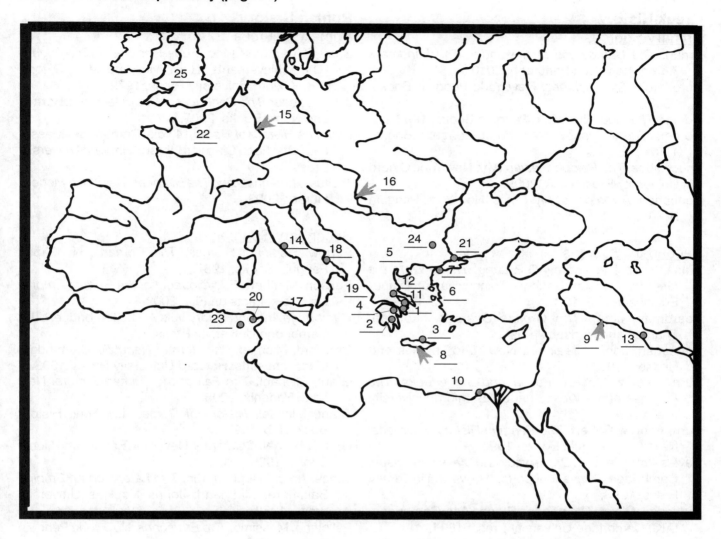

Selected References

Greek History

Primary Sources

Arrian. *The Campaigns of Alexander: The Landmark Arrain.* New York: Pantheon, 2010.

Herodotus. *The Histories.* New York: Penguin Books, 2003.

Homer. *The Iliad.* New York: Penguin Books, 1998.

Homer. *The Odyssey.* New York: Penguin Books, 1997.

Thucydides. *The Peloponnesian War.* New York: Oxford University Press USA, 2009.

Xenophon. *A History of My Times.* New York: Penguin Books, 1981.

Secondary Sources

Amos, Hugh and Andrew G.P. Lang. *These Were the Greeks.* Chester Springs, Pennsylvania: Dufour Editions Inc., 2010.

Boardman, John. *The Greeks Overseas.* London: Thames and Hudson, 1999.

Boardman, John. *Greek Art.* New York: Thames and Hudson, 1996.

Burn, Andrew Robert. *Persia and the Greeks: The Defense of the West.* London: Stanford University Press, 1984.

Burn, Andrew Robert. *The Penquin History of Greece.* New York: Penguin Books, 1990.

Davies, John Kenyon. *Democracy and Classical Greece.* Cambridge, Massachusetts: Harvard University Press, 1993.

Dickinson, Oliver. *The Aegean Bronze Age.* Cambridge, U.K.: Cambridge University Press, 1994.

Dinsmoor, William Bell. *The Architecture of Greece.* New York: W.W. Norton and Co., 1975.

Finley, Moses. *The Ancient Greeks.* New York: Penguin Books, 1987.

Huxley, George Leonard. *Early Sparta.* Cambridge, Massachusetts: Harvard University Press, 1970.

Jones, A. H. M. *Athenian Democracy.* Baltimore: John Hopkins University Press, 1986.

Kitto, H. D. F. *The Greeks.* Piscataway, New Jersey: Aldine Transaction, 2007.

Meiggs, Russel. *The Athenian Empire.* Oxford, U.K.: Oxford University Press, 1979.

Snodgrass, A.M. *The Dark Age of Greece.* New York: Routledge, 2000.

Wilcken, Ulrich. *Alexander the Great.* New York: W.W. Norton and Co., 1967.

Roman History

Primary Sources

Brunt, P.A. and J.M. Moore, eds. *Res Gestae Divi Augusti* [The Achievements of the Divine Augustus]. Oxford, U.K.: Oxford University Press, 1979.

Julius Caesar. *The Conquest of Gaul.* New York: Barnes and Noble Books, 2005.

Livy. *The History of Rome* 14 vols. Cambridge, Massachusetts: Loeb Classics Library, Harvard University Press.

Tacitus. *The Annals and The Histories.* New York, Modern Library, 2003.

Secondary Sources

Barrow, Reginald Haynes. *The Romans.* New York: Penguin Books, 1987.

Bunson, Matthew. *Encyclopedia of the Roman Empire.* New York: Facts on File, 2002.

Cambridge Ancient History, vols 7–12. Cambridge, U.K.: Cambridge University Press.

Crawford, Michael. *The Roman Republic.* Cambridge, Massachusetts: Harvard University Press, 1993.

Grant, Michael. *The Fall of the Roman Empire.* New York: Phoenix, 2005.

Grant, Michael. *History of Rome.* New York: History Book Club, 1997.

Grant, Michael. *Gladiators.* New York: Barnes and Noble Books, 1996.

Jones, Arnold Hugh Martin. *The Later Roman Empire.* Baltimore, Maryland: Johns Hopkins University press, 1986.

Pallottino, Massimo. *The Etruscans.* New York: Penguin Books, 1978.

Watson, George Ronald. *The Roman Soldier.* Ithaca, New York: Cornell University Press, 1985.

Webster, Graham. *The Roman Imperial Army.* Norman, Oklahoma: University of Oklahoma Press , 1998.

Wheeler, Mortimer. *Roman Art and Architecture.* New York: Thames and Hudson, 1985.

Wilkes, John. *The Roman Army.* Cambridge, U.K.: Cambridge University Press, 1986.